Why Do All the Locals Think We're Crazy?

Why Do All the Locals Think We're Crazy?

Three Men, Three Kayaks, the Caribbean
and One Bad Idea

≈≈≈≈≈

Scott Finazzo

Cover design by Scott Finazzo and Pixelstudio

Published in the U.S.

Edited by Jacqueline Nelson

Scott Finazzo

www.scottfinazzo.com

ISBN-13: 978-1496108500
ISBN-10: 1496108507

10 9 8 7 6 5 4 3 2 1

This book is dedicated to my sons:

Ryan, Nicholas, and Cameron Finazzo.

You are a constant adventure

and have given my life meaning beyond words.

The U.S. and British Virgin Islands

TABLE OF CONTENTS

FOREWORD 1

INTRODUCTION 0

CHAPTER 1

A Pebble Becomes a Boulder 0

CHAPTER 2

Setting Up Shop 14

CHAPTER 3

From the Plains to the Tropics 32

CHAPTER 4

The Plan (Almost) Comes Together 50

CHAPTER 5

Going Nowhere 68

CHAPTER 6

Crossing the Ocean 82

CHAPTER 7

The Adventure Takes a Turn 104

CHAPTER 8

On My Own 124

CHAPTER 9

An Unlikely Rescue 132

CHAPTER 10

Coming Apart and Coming Together 152

CHAPTER 11

What a Long, Strange Trip It's Been 168

Foreword

The story of my own solo kayak trip among the reefs and islands of the Caribbean began in a well-worn spiral-bound notebook in which I scribbled my journal entries each night by candlelight to the music of mosquitoes humming outside the nets. I mostly wrote those words for myself, to remember the details that would surely be forgotten if I had not attempted to record at least some of them. Bits of that journal were later summarized in a feature article for *Sea Kayaker*, and the thrill of seeing my words in print led me to believe I could turn those wax-splattered and DEET-stained pages into a book. The book did eventually get finished and published in 2005, fifteen years after the trip it described. *On Island Time: Kayaking the Caribbean* was my second book, and like the first, was published by University Press of Mississippi in my home state, with little likelihood of finding wide readership beyond the region. Other kayaking narratives of far more epic trips written by paddlers of far greater renown were still relatively unnoticed in the larger world of travel writing, but I'd read them all when planning my trip and I hoped that by publishing my own story I might inspire someone else to go have an adventure.

Little did I know that the book would find its way to the middle of Kansas, about as far as you can get from the ocean on an entire continent, and that it would give this crew you are about to meet here the audacity to believe they not only paddle the islands themselves, but that they could build their own boats in which to do it. Actually it was entirely the fault of the author whose misadventure you're about to read. His friends were simply coerced into it after he read my book and came up with this hare-brained scheme, and despite his best efforts, they all survived. It does make me wonder though, how many others reading the narrative of my impulsive adventure as a twenty-five year old already fed up with the rat race have attempted a similar stunt and simply disappeared at sea? How many others have made their way to the storm-lashed islands from Kansas, Nebraska, the Dakotas and other landlocked territories only to find themselves at the mercy of wind and wave? Did they all perish or will the world soon be inundated with their narratives, appearing out of nowhere just as this one has found its way into your hands? How many more like Finazzo will not be content to simply emulate my trip, but rather will pester me with questions about writing and publishing until at last I relent, spilling all the secrets likely to lead them into a more successful publishing career than my own?

But all kidding aside, I still find it remarkable that something I wrote so long ago, bit by bit, on beach after beach, led to an email out of the blue, that in turn led to a remarkable friendship with a fellow adventurer and a damn fine writer who no doubt has a bright future ahead. When you read this story you will both laugh at Finazzo's great sense of humor and you will learn things you didn't know from his observations from an island world Caribbean tourists never see from their posh hotels. But take this as a warning: you will also be inspired. You may even decide to do something foolish yourself. But if you do, I'm off the hook now. It's all Scott Finazzo's fault.

Scott B. Williams

May 14, 2014

Somewhere between the last boat and the next one…

INTRODUCTION

Grown men doing impractical things, regardless of common sense, is nothing new. Such occurrences can usually be traced back to a bar, a kitchen table, or a front porch: basically anywhere men gather socially and drink beer. One guy will toss down the last gulp or two of his Anheuser Busch product and say, "You know what we should do?" And that's when they begin. Shenanigans inevitably ensue. Our case is a rare exception. The idea was conceived completely sober, with sound mind and body.

At no time during our adventure, did I ever think my life was in danger. Let me just say that right off the bat. Even during the worst times, I don't recall ever thinking that I could die. Maybe because the islands were all in relatively close proximity, I felt a false sense of security. Maybe I just didn't take the time to truly consider the hazards. My experience on the ocean, up to that point, had been limited to cavorting in the waves near the shoreline on various vacations, and I certainly had no experience building boats. So when my friends and I concocted the plan to build boats, take them down to the Virgin Islands, and spend a few weeks exploring, warning alarms should have been going off in my head. Instead, my mind filled with vivid images of primitive and masculine exploration among picturesque tropical islands. Looking back with the clarity of hindsight, the failure wasn't necessarily just in the plan, but the execution.

In reality, anytime you're negotiating the temperamental ocean, you are gambling; and the odds are always with the house. The water is unpredictable and aggressive, there is abundant life that can be deceptively poisonous, and carnivores silently patrol their turf just below the surface. Factoring in all of those things, I should have been more afraid than I was. I think my confidence was a result of a combined stubbornness and ignorance. I was too focused on the romance of the idea to adequately evaluate my circumstances and too dumb to realize the danger. But I can honestly say, while kayaking the ocean through the Virgin Islands, my main fear was not injury or death, but losing my kayak to the sea causing the adventure to be over.

Two friends and I concocted a plan to build sea kayaks. We would ship them down to the Virgin Islands and explore. Even in retrospect, the idea sounds romantic and adventurous. That was certainly the appeal for us. We were at a collective point in our lives where routine had become a hushed governing force, and the notion of breaking out of the day-to-day grind in such an exotic location was more of a temptation than any of us could resist.

This adventure puzzle, however, was missing a few key pieces. First of all the "kayak" part was problematic. Due to logistical and budgetary issues we thought the best course of action would be to build them ourselves. My years of experience combined with all the boats the other two guys had built added up to a grand total of zero. None of us had ever so much as attempted to patch an inflatable raft, much less construct an entire boat. The same can be said about our boating skills on the ocean. We are firefighters from Kansas, which is a detail that could not put us further from being "boat builders" or "sea kayakers." In fact, one guy had never been in a kayak before in his life. As you're reading this, I'm sure that red flags are appearing faster than you can count. It seems so obvious now.

The journey would encompass everything we hoped and nothing we expected: wanderlust, adventure, debt, and bucket list items we didn't even know we had until they occurred. As you will read, the trip began with an idea that was more joke than an actual suggestion, which gave birth to a plan. The plan grew into a grand expedition that included a tropical setting, rum, laughs, terror, arguments, setbacks, a yacht full of inebriated Dutch airline pilots, a rescue at sea, more rum, the coast guard, strange naked beach children, struggle, and a measure of introspection only afforded people when they are removed from their comfort zone and forced to acknowledge their own mortality.

I completed this manuscript in the years following the trip. It has been a slow, sometimes painstaking process. As I wrote I looked back over my journal, pictures, and videos, recalling the sights with simultaneous joy and sadness. It was a defining moment in my life and the bond that developed between the three of us has been firmly and forever cemented.

Travel is an interesting undertaking. When you travel you take all of your baggage with you, and by baggage I don't mean suitcases. You take your experiences and your stress. You take happiness and pain. You take the story of you. And while you are away, particularly if you travel abroad, a metamorphosis happens. You think you are traveling to see new sights; but in fact, if you're doing it right, it is not the scenery but the experience that changes you. The story of who you were evolves into the story of who you are now. Travel is an exchange of experiences and, in the end, you receive as much as you give while you are away. When you return, you are kinder to those different than you, more patient with those who require patience, and appreciative of the blessings you have been given.

Two friends and I dared to dream. We weathered the snarky looks and predictions of failure. We broke free from the shackles of routine and challenged ourselves to do something that most could never fathom. We built boats, we took them to the Caribbean, and we chased a belief: a belief that growing older does not necessarily mean growing up. It wasn't easy, and there were doubts and regrets along the way; but on the other side of it, we were changed forever. Thanks for coming along with us on the journey.

"Because in the end you won't remember the time you spent working in the office or mowing your lawn. Climb that Goddamn mountain."

- Jack Kerouac

CHAPTER 1

A Pebble Becomes a Boulder

Even if only by the determining factors of DNA and age, I am a man. As I write this I am 37 ½ years old. The "1/2" is important because according to a Center for Disease Control and Prevention study, the life span of the American male is 75.2 years. That means that, as an average American male, I am EXACTLY at halftime (statistically speaking of course). I have considered the numbers and played the mental plus/minus game with myself. I add my general good health – plus. I work out on a fairly regular basis – plus. I drink – minus. Arguably more than I should – minus. I don't smoke – plus. They know me by name at Burger King – minus. You see how this works and it is obviously a pointless game because I won't know the final score until there's nothing I can do about it.

At roughly this point in life, men and women alike begin to experience certain realizations, revelations, and fears: the dreaded *mid-life crisis*. We've all seen this crisis manifest itself in the form of divorces, sports cars, tattoos, piercings, and awful wardrobe choices. You've seen these people and know exactly who I am talking about.

For myself, as my mid-thirties approached, I did not feel a "crisis" as much as an understanding that I wanted to experience as much as I could in my remaining years. I have a family, a career, a mortgage, credit card bills, a car payment, and everything else that goes along with a stereotypically Midwestern suburban existence. By most standards I am a face in the crowd. Despite those vanilla facts about me I do live in a very unique location. From my driveway, I can drive approximately ten hours in any direction and still be absolutely nowhere. I wanted more.

I am no stranger to coloring outside the lines but, all in all, my adventures have been relatively safe; relative being the operative word. My mother might argue with you, but true adventure seekers would see me as a novice. I have hiked mountains in the Rockies, gone SCUBA diving in Cancun and gone parasailing near Cozumel. I have gone swimming with the manatees in Florida, with sharks in Hawaii and The Bahamas, and with the stingrays in Grand Cayman. I have sailed across the Gulf of Mexico. I have been rappelling, skiing, rock climbing, mountain biking, running, and I even drove a rental car down into the heart of Times Square once. My occupation as a firefighter has drawn me into burning buildings and a variety of unsettling situations. It's been far from a boring life, yet, I still wanted more.

I have travelled enough, however, that my friends sometimes ask me to recommend vacations locations. Several years ago I was approached by a friend and co-worker about destination ideas for his honeymoon. My friend, Eric, knew that I had been to multiple places in the Caribbean and I could point him in the right direction for a perfect tropical honeymoon. Cancun is beautiful and inexpensive. Key West is awesome, popular, and unique but not as "tropical" as much as it is bars and retail. Puerto Rico has beautiful beaches and Jamaica is cool within the confines of the resorts but almost cliché as a honeymoon destination. There are many options. Because Eric is a good friend of mine, I pointed him in the direction of my happy place: the place whose images I keep in the "break in case of emergency" glass case of my mind to sustain me through Kansas winters. It is the place I love so much that I want to tell everyone who will listen, and yet I want to keep it a secret and all to myself. Well, it's hardly a secret. It is extremely popular (and for good reason) among sunshine worshiping tourists. I recommended they go to the Virgin Islands.

I had only been there once, but immediately fell deeply in love with the islands and felt an umbilical connection that keeps me wanting to return. There is something remote and exotic, yet warm and welcoming about the Virgin Islands. The U.S. Virgin Islands consist mainly of three islands: Saint Thomas, Saint John, and Saint Croix. Those, along with dozens of other smaller islands, total about 130 square miles. They were sold to the United States from Denmark in 1916 so we could effectively block the Germans from buying them and using them as a submarine nursery. Twenty five million dollars later (roughly equivalent to $435 million in 2014 dollars) America became the proud owners of some prime Caribbean real estate.

Following my recommendation, Eric and his wife Erin decided to go to St. Thomas to spend their honeymoon. They devoted their week to Bolongo Bay, St. Thomas and fell in love with the islands as I had.

Around the time of their trip I had read a review of a book by Scott B. Williams titled *On Island Time.* It is the story of Williams' solo kayak trip down the coast of Florida and across to the Caribbean islands. I was intrigued and, after some (not so) subtle hint dropping, my wife bought the book for me. I was completely taken by it. The adventure, the solitude, the danger, the thrill... all of it! I knew I would never be gutsy enough to attempt an open ocean crossing but... how *awesome* would that be?!?

I went on about the redundant monotony of a Midwestern life while keeping tucked away in the back of my mind, the clean slate on which I hoped to write my own adventure story. The problem was that this little idea of an epic adventure was not placed neatly away on a mental shelf. It became a pebble in my shoe: small and unassuming, yet could not be ignored.

Eric returned from his honeymoon with stories of clear water, beautiful beaches, and friendly islanders. He talked of places that I knew and loved, and it warmed my heart to hear the names and descriptions of those places that I keep in my mind all of the time. He was amazed, as was I, at the sheer number of islands and the close proximity in which they all lie. At numerous points, if you can find a rock to stand on, you can see several dozen islands and keys (or "cays" depending on who you talk to, which map you look at, or if you even care) speckled across the ocean in front of you.

In a semi-related conversation, I mentioned to him the book I had recently read about some guy who kayaked down the coast of Florida and through the Caribbean. I told Eric that even though I would never do that, I was intrigued by the testicular fortitude of that guy. Eric casually responded, "We should do that. We should fly down to St. Thomas and then spend a week or so kayaking the islands." We shared a few laughs, nods, and "that would be awesome" comments, and then moved on to less important conversation.

Remember the aforementioned pebble in my shoe? It had become a boulder, and that boulder was Eric's idea of kayaking the Virgin Islands. I did not want to do this. I *needed* to do this. It was a lazy constant distraction that lurked in my thoughts and dreams. I would hover in book stores around every published word related to this idea. I looked at survival books, Caribbean travel books, kayak books, etc. I killed time in outdoorsy type stores looking at tents and paddles and anything that could or should be used for an ocean kayak trip. I had become consumed. Being firefighters and being distracted is not really a good combination. For our safety and the safety of the public, we needed to flush out this idea.

The Boat

Eric and I spent several evenings at the fire station, sitting on the tailboard of a ladder truck, brainstorming ideas. The plan seemed simple enough. We would use the internet to find a place that would rent us kayaks for a week or so, fly down (taking only the things we would pack on the boats), and adventure and mayhem would commence. Step one would turn out to be strike one. In our search for rental kayaks we found many, but not the type of kayaks we needed. They were all the "sit on top kind" that the resorts rent by the hour to tourists. We needed bona fide sit-in, ocean kayaks.

Ironically we later found several locations on the islands that rent exactly the kind of kayaks we needed. But we didn't know this at the time. In hindsight, however, the better parts of this story involve the planning, building, transporting, construction, and return of our kayaks.

We spent hours and hours scouring the internet and travel books for ideas. We were getting nowhere in a hurry. Renting a kayak was no longer an option, but we were determined to carry out our plan. Our second thought was short lived. We could *buy* ocean kayaks and simply ship them down there and back when we were done. With this idea we would have had the added benefit of owning a kayak that we could reuse year after year, assuming we would pull it off, survive, and want to do it again. However, the type of kayaks we wanted to buy for the trip were around two thousand dollars each, which was FAR beyond what we initially had planned to spend to rent them. Shipping them down would cost about $600. That idea ended about as quickly as it began because, as I mentioned before, we are firefighters and do not have several grand to be tossing around on flighty ideas.

Even being mathematically challenged, that idea was not adding up. I was completely consumed by the thought of kayaking the islands, but planned on using both of my kidneys for as long as I could and was not keen on the idea of offering one up on eBay in order to finance a boat trip. Also, considering the fact this would certainly not be the last hairbrained idea in my lifetime, I would quickly run out of non-essential organs to put up for bid. We would not be buying kayaks for this trip.

While scrambling for alternative ideas, Eric stumbled across "folding" kayaks. Folding kayaks are basically boat kits. Anyone who has ever put together a tent has the general concept of the folding kayak. You assemble poles to create the frame and wrap it all in some sort of waterproof material (depending on manufacturer). We were on to something!

Eric approached me with what he had found. He gave me the details of the boats and listed all of their attributes, which led me to believe that these were just what we were looking for. The folding kayaks were the right length, the right size, and they folded down into cases or bags small enough to check onto an airplane. Ecstatic, I said, "Man! Sounds perfect! Can we buy these local or do we need to order online?"

Eric replied, reservedly, "uhhhh... online."

"Okay, not a big deal. How much are we talking?" I asked him. Eric giggled as I responded by curiously raising my eyebrows and protruding my bottom lip.

"About fifty-three hundred each," remarked Eric.

"Dollars?!?"'

"Yeah," responded Eric, giggling again. I remained silent. We did not buy fifty-three hundred dollar folding kayaks.

This is probably a good place to tell you a little bit about Eric. Eric "Frank" Gifford grew up on a Wyoming ranch. He came to work at the fire department about ten years ago and was assigned to my shift. His work ethic and sense of humor were a perfect fit and caused him to be instantly accepted. He has an engineer's mind, a mechanic's hands, and the maturity of a juvenile. He is dangerously smart. Imagine a cross between Stephen Hawking, John Belushi in *Animal House*, Bob Villa, and Raymond Babbit in *Rain Man*. We became quick friends.

Eric already had plan B (C or maybe even D if you're keeping score – I've lost track) prepared before he approached me with the five thousand dollar folding kayak idea. He had searched the web from top to bottom. I think he may have actually reached the end of the internet. He had found building plans to make "folding" kayaks. Against my better judgment, I nibbled at the bait and began to ask questions: How much will they cost to build? What will they be made of? How long will they take to build? Are they dependable? How much will they cost again? Have they been tested? Are the plans reliable? Are you freaking serious? And so on. I asked questions at a rapid fire pace, and Eric attacked each of them with the ferocity of a lion. He had done his homework. He had a plan in his head. He believed in the idea. He was insane. ...and I liked it.

According to Eric, the boats we were going to build would be constructed with an aircraft aluminum frame, high density polyethylene (picture a plastic cutting board and you can see high density polyethylene) bracing, and a PVC coated nylon skin (a thick tarp). His research suggested they could be built for around $250 each.

Have you ever waited in line for a roller coaster? I mean a BIG roller coaster. As you climb in the car and are trapped... er, buckled in, it occurs to you that this was a bad idea? There had been some disconnect between rational thought and action. That was the same feeling I felt when I told Eric, "I'm IN!"

<u>Me</u>

What had led me to this reckless moment? It is hard to say. Aside from an apparently insatiable and adventuresome wanderlust that has possessed me from an early age, I can only account for it by my long-time love affair with the ocean, which was set in motion many years previously after a series of significant events.

I am the married father of three boys with a long history of impulsively jumping at any opportunity to go to the beach. I have long felt a connection to salt water that is not easily explained. On the surface, my attachment doesn't make sense. I am a fair skinned Midwesterner who only truly feels at ease with sand in my flip flops and salty air in my face.

Jimmy Buffett has a song called "First Look" about the effects of his first exposure to the crystal clear waters of the Caribbean. Although my parents took me several times to the ocean as a kid, it was in 1998 that I had *my* first look. A very good friend of mine was married to a Navy officer stationed in Puerto Rico. She invited a buddy and me to come visit them. He and I flew from Kansas City to San Juan for my first plane ride over an ocean.

She picked us up from the airport and after a quick lunch we drove towards her home in Fajardo, stopping for a moment at

Luquillo Beach on the northern coast. We stepped out of the car into a slow motion moment of reverence. The three of us stood in silence. Bob Marley's voice rang out from a boom box in the sand near a group of teenagers playing in the shallow, pounding surf; it was almost as if the locals had seen the Americans coming and wanted to perpetuate the stereotypes. The water was a half a dozen shades of clear. Palm trees danced in the wind. I was completely taken and I have not been the same since. From that single moment, I have been changed. I cannot be away from the warm waters of the Caribbean for any length of time without feeling that my gills are drying up.

Fast forward ten years and the perfect storm occurred: my wife bought me Scott B. Williams' book, Eric took a trip to St. Thomas, and an idea was born. Once Eric and I had ironed out some of the wrinkles and the trip had transitioned from an idea to a genuine possibility, I needed to inform my family. Not knowing whether to ask, tell, or simply post a note on the day I would leave, I sauntered into the kitchen. The entire family had assembled in preparation for dinner. In a moment of decisive indecision I chose to lob my intentions into the middle of the room and brace for impact.

"I am going to go to the Virgin Islands with a few guys from work. We are going to build kayaks and ship them down. We will spend a week or two paddling from island to island, exploring uninhabited islands, and sleeping in tents."

With remarkable calm, Amy replied, "Have any of you built boats before?"

"No, but Gifford has a plan."

"Have any of you been kayaking on the ocean before?"

"No. In fact, John has never been in a kayak before in his life."

My oldest son Ryan, apathetic to the entire conversation, interrupted, "When is dinner going to be ready?"

Amy replied, "Soon. So, you guys are really going to do this?"

My other two sons, Nicholas and Cameron, equally as apathetic as their older brother added, "What are we having?"

I turned to them with a puzzled look wondering if they had heard a single word of the conversation.

Amy asked coolly, "Am I still your life insurance beneficiary?"

"Yes. You will get the money if I die."

"OK, then. Have fun. Boys, dinner is ready. Eat quickly because I need to go pick out a new car. Scott, can you give me a ball park idea what the death benefit is on your policy?"

No one in my family was surprised at my idea. My history of dumb adventures was nothing new. A small part of me would have liked to see at least a little bit of concern. The greater part of me was proud of the fact that, in most households, the aforementioned conversation would have sent shockwaves felt throughout the neighborhood. My family knows that if I have the opportunity to climb a mountain or play in the ocean, I am likely going to take it. I took their apathy as silent support.

The Cast

Eric and I wanted to share our great idea and adventure with some inner circle, mutual friends. And by "share our great idea and adventure" I mean add to the number of participants, thus increasing our chances that one of us would be able to swim or paddle for help, which would be an almost certain need.

While considering our respective roster of possible players, we needed to consider interest, ability to work, ability to play, mental flexibility, and sense of humor. Eric and I carefully evaluated every name on the list and graded them on a one to ten scale in each category then plotted the results on a z-score chart to find an approximation for a binomial distribution. ...Okay, that's not exactly true. In all honesty, I don't even know what most of those words mean. Actually we picked a handful of our closest friends that we thought were adventurous and crazy enough to attempt the trip and just asked.

Many were intrigued but very few actually showed more than what can only be described as morbid curiosity. For most it was a financial no, a "no possible way on God's green earth will my wife let me go" no, a bad timing no, or a "not only no, but HELL NO" no. Only two were willing to step up to the plate.

Participant Number Three: John "Heff" Heffernon was born and raised in the Midwest. He grew up working in his father's bar and graduated from the University of Kansas with some degree that probably does very little to help him advance in his current career as a firefighter. John likes to work hard and relax harder. He is also a gambler, not just on the casino floor but in many aspects of life. That should explain his interest in this adventure. In fact, I don't think it was the draw of the physical challenge or the promise of beautiful tropical beaches, but more the test of getting permission and the blessing of his wife and two daughters. He bucked the odds and was able to pull it off. Not only did he get the blessing from his family, but his wife, Vicky, was charitable (read: foolish) enough to allow us to use their garage as our primary workshop.

Final Participant: Keith Murry has been the captain (boss) to each of us individually at the fire station, as well as all together as a shift. He has been our fire department mentor. Keith is a rural type of guy who has a wife and two daughters, acres of land, horses, pigs, tractors, a windmill, and an array of other farm and hunting things that could not interest me less. But Keith is an extremely smart guy who is quick witted and half crazy. Are you seeing a pattern? Another piece of the puzzle fell right into place.

Keith Murry and John Heffernon were on board. Being firefighters as well, we knew that we were all similar enough to be able to tolerate each other for days on end, yet different enough to each bring something to the table. It all came together in a glorious swan dive into the pool of insanity. Eric and I had decided on our boats and found a couple of fools to complete the ensemble. The cast was complete!

The Plan

To the typical tourist, the Virgin Islands are a collection of random resorts with magnificent beaches and breathtaking panoramic views. Anyone who dares to venture out of the full service, homogenized, cookie cutter, tourist trap hotels knows that the islands are alive: each one similar yet unique. For us, the draw was their natural beauty, the relatively calm water, and the abundance of small keys in close proximity to one another.

The trip would have to start in Charlotte Amalie, St. Thomas. What once was a haven for pirates is now the bustling capital of the U.S. Virgin Islands. It is a popular cruise ship destination and the location for the primary airport in the Lesser Antilles. Our thought was to spend one travel day from Kansas City to St. Thomas, spend the night in Charlotte Amalie, and then taxi and ferry our way to our starting point.

We downloaded several maps of the U.S. and British Virgin Islands. There were many places we had either been or heard about that we wanted to see. If we were to place push pins in the map on the locations that we *wanted* to visit, it would look like one of us had taken a handful of them and done a full Nolan Ryan wind up and pitch into the map. There was no practical way to plan a route that would enable us to visit all of these places in the short amount of time we would be there.

In a rare moment of common sense, we decided to eliminate the "want to see" factors and simplified things by choosing a logical route for beginners. We decided to ferry from St. Thomas to the eastern most end of the British islands and kayak our way back west towards the U.S. side. We chose our route along the southern edge of the British islands. A launch from the eastern shores of Virgin Gorda would get us started.

Virgin Gorda, at approximately eight square miles, is the third largest of the British islands. It was allegedly named by Christopher Columbus because he thought the profile of the island looked like a fat woman lying down. Having seen the island once before, if I squint my eyes, kind of turn my head to the side and use my imagination, I guess I can see it. Like many of the islands in the Caribbean, Virgin Gorda has a checkered past. It has had a roster of seedy inhabitants including Blackbeard and Captain Kidd. Pirates would hide out in the waters surrounding Virgin Gorda and plunder Spanish galleons trying to slip through the calm Caribbean waters.

The population of Virgin Gorda surged in the seventeenth century when the plantation sugar industry flourished. Plantation slaves discovered that an interesting by-product of the sugar refining process, molasses, could be fermented into alcohol. A little distillation, removal of the impurities, and *voila*... rum. Rum became a valuable commodity to pirates and privateers alike and has been a Caribbean staple ever since, being used for everything from cures to currency. In 1838, slavery was abolished and the economy took a hit. Apparently when your "property" doesn't include humans and you are required to pay your workers, the bottom line suffers. After a few decades of recovery, things began to turn around and, by way of a controlled tourism industry, the Virgin Gorda economy is hovering in a comfortable middle ground where the tourist dollar strongly supports, but doesn't rule it.

Virgin Gorda would be our starting point. There is a campground on the eastern coast where we could set up camp and assemble the kayaks. Rather than fly with a week's worth of rations, we decided we would gamble and assume there would be a market or grocery store on the island where we could get water and food supplies for the trip. If you're going to gamble, why not gamble on the few items critical and necessary for survival? Makes sense, right?

From there, the plan was to spend the next seven days meandering our way around Ginger, Cooper, Salt, Peter, and Norman Islands along with a bread crumb trail of smaller islands and rocks all leading us back to the U.S. islands.

We were four guys from Kansas with zero boat building experience who had decided to build kayaks. We same four guys, who had never kayaked on the ocean, were going to take our self-built boats to sea. We would paddle from island to island and begin each day with no real idea how it would end. In hindsight, I can see why some people laughed at us when we discussed the trip, and I understand why immediate family members upped our life insurance policies. None of our plans made practical sense, but the lure of the adventure had proven too strong to resist. We were going to go to the Caribbean.

CHAPTER 2

Setting Up Shop

The *Inuit* are varying groups of people with similar cultures that are indigenous to the arctic portion of the world. They are the ones who live up in the icebox of the planet; where the average winter temperature is a brisk forty below zero. Winter is dark there. Near the North Pole the darkness lasts from approximately October to March. This is the polar opposite of my "happy place." When most people imagine hell, they typically conjure up images of demons scurrying around in flames and brimstone. My hell is basically the icy tundra that I just described above. I do not believe Satan is a fork tongued demon with horns and a pitchfork, but rather a parka wrapped Mephistopheles scoundrel with bad breath, wearing Crocks and standing in a frozen wasteland listening to U2 as he welcomes me to my nightmare.

The male *Inuk*, who is primarily responsible for the manly things like hunting and fishing, is forced to become extremely familiar with the frigid arctic waters in order to gather food to survive. If you are picturing the stereotypical image of an Eskimo, you pretty much have the idea of an Inuk. In order to harvest the bounty contained in their frigid waters, the Inuit people developed a single passenger boat made of a wooden frame wrapped in seal skin called a *qajaq*. Those boats were extremely buoyant and easily maneuverable in the water, perfect for Inuks gathering meals for the village.

Over time, the rest of the world caught on to the design and continues to produce variations of the Inuit vessel under the name "kayak," which means "man's boat" or "hunter's boat." The four of us would not be putting a dent in any wildlife population and our "manliness" may not be on a par with the average Inuk, but we were going to build kayaks.

Eric, being the brains of the operation, had scoured the internet and found many websites discussing the economic benefits and ease of building your own kayak. A few even offered free plans for kayak construction. He found one in particular that caught his attention. It offered design plans and testimonies. Eric even went as far as contacting the website host to thoroughly interrogate him about the boats. Having heard what he wanted to hear, Eric took the next step.

"I built the kayak," Eric said to me abruptly one morning as we were walking into the fire station to report for duty.

"Are you serious?" I asked in obvious disbelief.

"Kind of."

What he had done was download the plans, bought a hundred feet of dowel rods, and used the rods and cardboard to build a replica of what our kayaks would look like. He invited us over the following morning to see what he had done, so we could get a rough idea of what we were getting into.

The next day, on a cool January morning, Eric opened the door allowing John and I into his house. Just inside the door was his creation. He had certainly built a replica of a kayak. When I say "built a replica," I don't mean he constructed a model on his kitchen table that we could pick up and scrutinize. Eric had built a full "to scale" eighteen foot wooden stick kayak in his living room. It sat at an angle because it was too long to fit conveniently in the quaint and otherwise very nice living room.

The model was a monstrosity and it was beautiful. Its elegant contours came to a point at either end. Although crude and elementary, the curves were profoundly feminine in the same way a Fender Stratocaster recalls the curves of a woman's body. But, instead of the sleek ash body of a strat, we were looking at birch sticks held together with duct tape and pieces of a bulk toilet paper box.

Eric walked around it explaining what would be needed to make the real kayak and how we would go about building it. He wanted to make some minor design changes and had already researched where to buy the major supplies. Understanding the absurdity of this next statement, I will say it anyway: it made sense. While puzzled at how exactly that popsicle stick kayak would become a seaworthy vessel, John and I cautiously gave our approval to move forward. We both knew Eric was a few donuts short of a dozen, but we completely trusted him and that would not waver throughout the entire adventure.

Not wanting to waste any time, we jumped right in and began setting aside days to commit to construction. We walked out of Eric's house that January morning and started work immediately. ...in May.

The Puzzle Pieces Come Together

It should come as no surprise when I say that building a kayak is not exactly rocket science. I can easily make that claim because Eric did all of the research and mental calculations to figure out how to build them; so for me, up to that point, the process was relatively simple. But there was a certain *bravado* about the whole process. We would be working in a garage with friends, surrounded by tools and empty beer cans. We were using our own hands and our own design to create something. It was bigger than the boats themselves. It was each of us planting a phallus flag at the threshold of our middle life. It was a statement saying, "I am here! I am a man and I refuse to resign myself to routine!" So we began.

The pre-construction phase was spent taking care of the basics. Keith and Eric raided one of Keith's barns and gathered the materials to build a "strongback," which is a cool sounding term for a bunch of short boards screwed together to make one long board where the varying incarnations of the kayaks would be secured while we put them together. It looked like a balance beam and would eventually be clamped to sawhorses and occupy the length of John's garage.

On sheets of poster board, Eric engineered lines and angles and numbers that defined rough outlines of what would become the high density polyethylene bracing. Put another way, he drew picture stencils of the plastic cutting board material "bones" of the boats. They would eventually become one of the more costly and frustrating parts of the construction process.

The first order of aluminum arrived at Eric's house. I can only imagine him tearing into those boxes with the fervor of a child on Christmas morning. He needed to ensure that we had received what we ordered and had ordered what we needed. Once he was satisfied with the delivery, he hopped into his old Toyota pickup truck and headed out to buy a new pipe cutter, a rivet gun, rivets, markers, drill bits, and anything else he could think of that would be needed to get the ball rolling.

The slightly beat-up cardboard box, shipped from Texas, contained lengths of aircraft aluminum that would soon be custom cut and then re-cut (and, more often than not, thrown away, cut, and re-cut again). The aircraft aluminum was chosen because of its high strength to low weight ratio. The pieces we received were six feet long and ½" in diameter - roughly as big around as your thumb.

In the following days, we set up shop in John's garage. Cars were moved outside, bikes were jammed into the corner, and all other assorted garage paraphernalia were tucked neatly into any available space in the perimeter of the garage. We had the parts that would become the boats and simply needed two more elements in order to begin: Eric and I moved in our toolboxes and we put beer in the refrigerator. Ready. Henry Ford's vision of the assembly line had been bastardized and re-imagined in the form of a four man kayak operation in a garage in Shawnee, Kansas. I'm sure Mr. Ford was up there somewhere smiling with pride, or more likely not.

Construction Begins

You should know I'm not built to be a morning person. I can appreciate the peaceful morning moments before the hectic pace of the day begins, but I am not at my best. I tend to start out slow and gain momentum throughout the day. There is a slow build that typically occurs - not necessarily in pace, but in my interest and contribution. As the day progresses, I experience an increasing, intrinsic inspiration. Creativity peaks. Output peaks. If my day were laid out in a line chart, you would probably see a spike in the late afternoon and another in the late evening. It is no different whether I am at work, on vacation, or building a kayak. Therefore, Eric knew not to expect a burst of productivity from me until I had a few hours of daylight behind me.

Yet, regularly, once we started construction, the cool, quiet mornings of John's subdivision were interrupted by the low rumble of the automatic door opener raising John's garage door and announcing our arrival. John's neighborhood is a typical upper middle class suburb. The streets are lined with very nice, fairly new houses, all with beautifully manicured lawns (if only to avoid the wrath of the homeowner's association). Our industry in John's garage was never a quiet, sedate affair. I can only assume the growling of the garage door opener had the same effect on the neighbors that the Federal Q siren had during World War II when it would wail its warning of an air raid. As the door raised, children were rushed from their half eaten breakfasts, pets were brought inside, and phone conversations were brought to an abrupt halt with, "I gotta go." I think it's safe to say that John did not endear himself to his neighbors that summer.

The first day was awkward. Four men assembled in a garage full of metal and tools, and only Eric had a clue as to what to do. Keith was a close second in comprehending the whole project. He is a smart man who could truly envision the ideas as Eric explained them. John and I nodded as if we understood; but in our heads, we were simply wondering if the beer was cold yet and if opening one at 9:00 a.m. could begin a pattern that would ultimately require an intervention.

At first, there was more discussion than action. Eric described in detail the plan and what we hoped to accomplish that day. Keith immediately went to work in a whirlwind of purposeful progress. John and I stood motionless and nodded at Eric's explanation. Eric recognized that he may as well have been talking in Mandarin to a sofa. He then slowed down and reiterated what he wanted to be accomplished. Finally, in utter frustration, he handed me a tape measure, a pipe cutter, and a section of aluminum.

"You. Measure. Cut. Got it?"

Now *that* I could understand! John received similar instructions, and we went to work. If you've ever given more than simple instructions to a child, you will understand what Eric and Keith had to endure. About every thirty seconds, John or I would turn to Eric and ask, "Like this?" or "Cut here?" Eric was forced to bite his tongue and gave preschool compliments as he patted us on the head and offered an encouraging, "Very good."

The tasks were simple enough. John and I took the six foot lengths of aluminum and cut them down to shorter, predetermined lengths according to what Eric wanted. Measure, mark, measure again, cut, and repeat. Keith and Eric used a band saw to carefully cut the polyethylene into exact geometric designed bracing or "bones." We agreed to build one kayak, then once we had figured out the learning curve of construction, we would build the rest of them simultaneously.

Construction days would all begin the same way. We wandered around the garage trying to re-acclimate ourselves to what was what and where we left off the day before. Eric made a mental plan of the day and what he wanted to accomplish as John and I drank energy drinks and wondered if those pieces of plastic and metal were ever going to form anything resembling a boat.

Struggling to Gain Momentum

Progress was slow, but even the tiniest steps forward were bringing us a little bit closer to our goal. Random friends or co-workers who stopped by would distort their faces in a look that appeared as if they were watching a slow motion train wreck. They would ask a lot of questions and respond with a side to side head shake, a chuckle, and an "o-ho-kay" with upward inflection on the "kay," so it was more of a question than a statement. To some, this barrage of doubts and questions might have been frustrating and considered condescending; to us, it became motivation.

    With every "You're crazy," "Are you serious," and "You guys are WAY too stupid to pull this off," our determination grew. It grew with the understanding that they were all correct, but we were going to accomplish what we set out to do regardless. We had called our shot. We were Babe Ruth who, according to legend, stood in the batter's box in the fifth inning of game three during the 1932 World Series and pointed to the center field bleachers. On the very next pitch, he sent the ball screaming over the center field wall. The four of us had grabbed a toolbox and an idea, stood in an empty garage, and pointed south east towards the Caribbean, and everyone in our circles had witnessed it. We had better send the ball over the fence, or we would lose any credibility we had and become a punch line. We could feel the pressure and, with all eyes on us, we forged ahead.

    The summer months arrived and days were passing us exponentially. The speed at which time was passing and the pressure of an immovable departure date combined into a palpable weight that was constant. The fuel to our fires was the visual progress. We cut the bones out of solid sheets of plastic. We joined the lengths of aluminum, and as we put the pieces together, they were actually starting to form what could, at some point, *kind of* LOOK like a boat! At any given time during the building process, John's neighbors would slow as they passed in their minivans and sport utility vehicles to cast curious looks at the random metal configurations decorating the driveway.

    The first boat came together as what can only be described as Frankenstein-ish. It had the shape of a beautiful, 18 foot kayak; but upon closer inspection you could see rivet misfires, aluminum that was cut too short and patched together with other pieces, and polyethylene braces that stuck out in places that shouldn't. The first kayak was rough. It was decided early on (I'm guessing on a day that I wasn't there to vote) that this first kayak would be mine. I was okay with that because it meant that as long as one of us claimed Frankenboat, we could advance on to building the rest.

For most adults, a garage is not only a convenient location to park and protect your vehicle, but also a place to store things. You store things like tools, lawn mowers, camping gear, and the extra sofa that your brother is going to pick up at some point. You pile up trash bags full of clothes that will go in the garage sale someday, boxes of old toys that will be donated to charity, pictures, pets, and everything else that doesn't fit conveniently into the higher visibility parts of your home. John's garage was no different.

On one particular day, John made the mistake of going to run errands while leaving us alone in his garage. If you don't know any firemen, allow me to enlighten you. We are children. Sure, we appear mature on the surface. We have a responsible job, after all. Most of us have experienced more death and destruction than any single human being should. I've read that humor is used as a coping mechanism. I don't know if humor is a means of coping or if the kids that want to grow up and ride on the big red truck may simply not evolve as most adults do. Regardless of the reason, we couldn't let the opportunity of being alone with John's things go to waste. Keith, typically the devious "idea" guy, drew our attention to the chandelier sitting in the corner of the garage. It was probably intended to go to a charity or, more appropriately, the trash.

"We should upgrade John's garage lighting. Let's hang the chandelier," he said. Without a verbal response, I laughed, set my drill down, and grabbed the ladder. Keith and I scurried up the ladder to John's garage lighting fixture and within minutes had removed the standard exposed single light bulb and installed a giant brass chandelier. John would surely become the envy of the neighborhood with his elegant and ostentatious garage illumination. There was no need to say the words. The expression on John's face when he arrived home was thanks enough.

And Then There Were Three

John and I both have active children, so putting in extra time building boats was a random luxury that did not occur very often. Many times during a morning or afternoon work session, one of us had to leave to drop off, pick up, or post bail for one of our kids. Eric was the constant. He battled several bouts of illness and many bouts with his wife because his duties at home were being severely neglected. Eric and John live in close proximity to one another; and John, in a glaring moment of inattentiveness, was foolish enough to give us his garage door security code. There were several evenings that John would hear the familiar yet surprising sound of his garage door being raised. Eric showed up on many nights, days, evenings, weekends, holidays, and any other time that you can imagine to work on the kayaks. He became a temporary member of the family. Eric was not only the brains, he was also the workhorse. He put in twice as many hours and at least twice as much money as John and I did. We were still behind schedule, and Eric was determined to get the boats done. It wasn't unusual for me to receive a text message with an update of what Eric had accomplished during a random visit to John's house.

It was late summer when Keith sustained a shoulder injury. He was bailing hay or some other irrelevant task that was probably very important to him and his family, but was in no way conducive to making the kayak trip a reality. He was forced to back out of the trip. That came as a blow on several levels. First, we were counting on his brains and hands during the building process. Second, with Keith's departure the IQ of participants dropped substantially. Up to that point the scale was balanced, but with Keith out, the dumb side became the majority; and Eric was forced to carry even more of the burden of responsibility to make sure the kayaks were built correctly. Third, and most importantly, Keith is a great guy and his presence would be missed.

Undeterred, Our Heroes Forge Ahead.

September was coming to a close, and our October 8th departure was approaching faster than we had anticipated. The subtle pressure that had been building had become a ringing in our ears: nagging and inescapable. Our exact completion date of "mid-summer" had come and gone, and the boat construction was still "in progress". At this point we had three kayaks. Each was eighteen feet long, made of metal, held in place by high density plastic, and joined by screws and rivets. For all intents and purposes, they were kayaks. We simply needed to add skins to them.

Months before, during a discussion over adult beverages, Eric brought us skin color options. We unanimously decided that we would make the bottoms black, and the tops would be a unique color of our choice. I chose red, mostly because of its symbolic association with the fire service. Eric chose orange and John chose yellow.

Once again we began with the Frankenboat. It was turned upside down, and the black PVC coated nylon was draped over and cut to Eric's specifications. We used a leather hole punch to create holes about two inches apart in the black nylon down both sides of the boat. We then took string and threaded the two sides together, back and forth in a criss-cross pattern, for the length of the boat until the nylon was pulled snug. It looked like a nautical corset; form fitting and sexy, yet straining with the potential for a catastrophic failure at any moment.

We then flipped it over and, with a specific type of vinyl cement glue that will come into play again soon, attached the red top to the black bottom. We painted on one coat of glue, let it dry, then painted on a second coat, and stuck on the red top. We used a heat gun to increase bond strength by the formation of cross-links in the polymer after solidification. Now, take two aspirin for the headache and I will translate: the heat gun made the glue stronger.

Eric single handedly cut open the red top skin to create the cockpit opening (the hole in the top of the kayak) and built the combing (the ring around the hole in the top of the kayak). He sliced into the skin with the surgical precision of a drunk, blind hibachi chef. With each cut, I cringed. I understood that he knew what he was doing, but I couldn't help but think he was destroying what we had come so close to completing. In fact, I became so uneasy about this, I finally had to put down my beer and get out of the chair in which I had become so comfortably ensconced and could no longer sit with my feet propped up and watch him (Sometimes my greatest contributions came in the form of not contributing.).

I paced back and forth like an expectant father. John, being more laid-back than I, wandered in and out of his house in such a nonchalant fashion that it almost annoyed me. He should have been every bit as nervous as I. He wasn't. His attitude was good either way. If the boats didn't get built, we would still go to the Virgin Islands for a week or so and no longer have to paddle from place to place. His optimistic ambivalence was counterproductive to hitting our deadline, but absolutely correct.

The cockpit and combing evolved from the appearance of a complete disaster to looking... *good*. Not just good; by the time Eric was finished, the boat looked fantastic. It looked like a usable, seaworthy kayak! With a few minor additions, like a seat, Frankenboat would be ready!

The Bottom Nearly Drops Out

As with any construction project, the major work is done at the beginning; but the progress isn't really felt until the project takes shape and looks like the final form.   With my boat completed, the work had become fun again.   The departure date was approaching, but we, for all intents and purposes, had one boat down and were in the home stretch with the other two.   We simply needed to add the skin to Eric's and John's boats.   Despite his injury and withdrawal from the trip, Keith was showing up to help; and there was a feeling of propulsion heading into the final week prior to departure.   I should have known better, but I began to feel everything finally coming together.   It was at that point, as we were beginning to glue John's skin together, that Eric uttered a string of words that sent me into catastrophic denial.

"We're not going to have enough glue to finish," he said in a moment of desperate surrender.   "This is our last can, and I can't get any more here in time.   I don't know what in the hell we're going to do," he muttered as he pitched his glue brush out into the yard.   He threw his hands up, shook his head, and walked out alone into the driveway where he paced.   I had had my moments of doubt before, but this was the first time I truly felt we were sunk.   We couldn't duct tape the boats.   We couldn't use just any glue.   We needed very specific glue for our very specific purpose.   We needed HH-66 vinyl cement glue, and we were out.

With every, "Did you try…" I asked, I was hit with progressively angrier, "Yes. Yes. YES! I've fucking tried everything!" I was desperate, and Eric was angry.

A Game Changing Mistake

My cousin Matt was getting married near St Louis, Missouri in my hometown of Granite City, Illinois that week. Eric optimistically told me I should go, and he would figure something

out about the glue. My family and I loaded up the car and headed
east on I-70. As the miles clicked away, my head was spinning. I
knew Eric had already exhausted all of his resources; and, though
he hadn't thrown in the towel yet, it was firmly in hand and he was
starting his wind up. I was worried and consumed with our
predicament.

Rarely, on a road trip, will I surrender the steering wheel,
but my wife was gracious enough to take over so I could try to
locate some damn glue. I was burning up my cell phone trying to
pinpoint any place in the St Louis area that would be open on a
Saturday night or Sunday that just might have a few cans of HH-
66. Every attempt I made was a maddening dead end. My head
began to throb at the thought of getting 2 ½ of our 3 boats finished
before the buzzer sounded and we had to board the plane sans
kayaks. We were beaten, and there was nothing I could do about
it.

Running behind schedule for the wedding, we were going
to have to go straight to the church and get dressed in the
bathroom. I have traversed Missouri taking the I-70 Kansas City
to St Louis route countless times since I was a kid and could make
the drive in my sleep. We were approaching our destination when
I had a hunch. I told Amy that the next exit might be a shortcut to
the church. She foolishly had blind faith in my suggestion and
didn't question my idea. We took the exit. Just as we passed the
point of no return where we could not cross back onto the
highway, I realized that we were not at the exit I thought we were.
Typically, I do not cuss in front of my children. This was a special
occasion which contained just the right stress ingredients that
called for a loud and proud F bomb. I let 'er fly and threw my
head back into the seat, closed my eyes, and took a deep breath.

I lowered my head back down and reluctantly eased open
my eyes. Something caught my eye. Just off the exit ramp was a

large metal building with the giant words across it that read "Tri City Canvas". "Amy, do you think there's any chance at all that that place has the glue I need?" In yet another show of unwavering support she said, "Let's find out."

She pulled into the gravel parking lot and Tri City Canvas looked deserted. All doors appeared to be closed, and only a few cars could be seen anywhere near the building. The posted hours stated exactly what I expected to see. They were closed and would not open again until Monday. I turned to walk back to the car when I noticed a partially opened door. I stuck my head in and spotted a lone man working. I let myself in and approached him inquiring whether they were open or not. "Well... not really. I'm just taking care of a few odds and ends," he said.

I explained my predicament and asked if there was any chance that he had any type of vinyl cement. He told me he did but only one kind: HH-66. A wrong turn had led me to a business that should have been closed where one man, who should not have been there, just happened to be staying late, and he told me he sold only one kind of cement: the exact kind I needed. A wave of excitement rolled over me. You would have thought I had won the lottery. I did my best to contain my elation as I bought three cans without asking or caring what the cost was. We were back on track! I couldn't get out to the car and call Eric fast enough!

Within days we were back in full production. Our time frame had shrunk from a year to months to weeks and finally to days. The last days were hectic and the nights were exhausting. The last seventy two hours were a dizzying whirlwind of activity.

On the morning of October 7th, the morning before our planes were taking off, I dropped my boys off at school, stopped for a caffeinated beverage, and with an anxious stomach drove my car to John's house. Eric already had the doors up, and it looked like he had been there working all night. The kayaks were out, the tools were out, he was undoubtedly on task. I strolled up the driveway and tossed a cheerful "good morning" grenade into the middle of his work area. He never even looked up at me as he deflected my greeting with an icy, "hey."

Within an hour John, Keith, Eric, Eric's wife Erin, and I were cutting and gluing and measuring and riveting while racing against a clock whose ticks were becoming louder with each passing second.

During the entire construction process I had been juggling work, family, friends, responsibilities, and boat building. I was doing everything I could to keep all of my plates spinning atop their sticks, making every effort to avoid the grand finale failure when they all come crashing down. By evening, all of my plates were wobbling. I received a phone call from my middle son who stated that he would be the starting quarterback in his football game that night. I told everyone, "Hey, I'm sorry, but Nick is starting QB tonight and I can't miss it. So I gotta run, but I'll be back right after the game."

You know that scene in the movie when the digital time bomb clicks down second by second? The background soundtrack builds tension into a crescendo and the clock reaches all zeroes; there is that moment of complete silence and then.... BOOM! Eric had had it! The burden and the frustration had been cumulative and had erupted. He had put in ungodly hours trying to make our dream a reality, and I had been coming and going every day trying to be everything to everyone. The time bomb exploded. He slammed a pair of pliers into the driveway and unleashed a string of expletives at me that encompassed everything from my work ethic to my mother's shitty taste in music. I, being in a pressure cooker myself, unleashed right back. It was a white trash altercation of epic proportions. Curse words and verbal jabs were being exchanged at such a rapid fire rate that, in an effort to outdo him, I think I even inadvertently created my own words and phrases that made absolutely no sense: "...and your fuckknuckle face can suck shit!"

The conflict never became physical, and I, regretfully, didn't go to my son's game. I stayed, and we all worked in virtual silence for the next several hours. The tension was palpable. Tools and boats were slammed around, and frustrations were mumbled to no one in particular.

The sun was sinking into the horizon as we glued the last deck lashing strap onto the boats. We had done it! Three boats were built and ready to be shipped down to the Virgin Islands. Because of the tension of the day and the fact that we were simply worn thin, there was no celebration. Oh, and there were the tiny, probably insignificant facts that we had never taken them apart and put them back together, they had never touched water, and the glue would be drying on the airplane. We didn't care. We were mentally and physically exhausted. In less than twenty four hours we would be in paradise; but at that moment, I just wanted to pack my things and leave. So that's what I did. I took my kayak apart, loaded it into the canvas bag, and drove home in silence.

The past year had been a roller coaster ride and the journey was certainly trying on many levels. It seemed like decades had passed since I had seen the dowel rod kayak model in Eric's living room. We had spent countless days and dollars putting those boats together, and I was driving home at 10:00 p.m. the night before our journey with an eighteen foot kayak folded down into a canvas bag in the back of my car.

At home my family was asleep. I opened a beer and spent about twenty minutes organizing my things for the trip and ensuring I had everything packed and accounted for. I placed my bags in a semi-organized pile, took one last look, and turned off the light. With a dull ache between my temples, I went to bed.

CHAPTER 3

From the Plains to the Tropics

My typical day begins when the early morning silence is shattered with repetitive blasts from my alarm clock. My pulse quickens and I grumble a sound that can only be described as something you might hear from a wounded badger. I am entirely capable of locating and pressing the snooze button with precision without even opening an eye. I'm good. After a few rounds of self-defeating snooze hockey, I roll out of bed and begin my morning routine, hardly cracking an eyelid.

Departure mornings are different. There is an underlying excitement residing just below the suspended consciousness. The alarm clock sounds and I reach beyond the snooze button straight for the on/off button. I take a deep breath and levitate out of bed. There's no need for last minute packing because the night before any trip my bags are packed and placed near the front door in the cocked and loaded position.

Depending on the location and duration of the trip, the "go pile" can have several different looks. The one consistent item is my trusty Jansport army green backpack. I bought it several years ago for my first trip to the Virgin Islands. Since then it has accompanied me on every vacation and misadventure I have pursued. It is my carry on for every single flight and on every single flight it is loaded with the same things:

- Passport
- Notebook and pen
- Two books (the paper and ink kind)
- One magazine
- iPod and headphones
- Phone charger
- Two packs of varying snacks
- Digital camera
- Gum

Rarely do I go anywhere requiring a passport, but I still take it with me for several reasons. First of all, it simply makes me feel like a real traveler. Secondly, as expensive as they are to obtain, I use the passport as identification at every opportunity. Just ask the cashier at the gas station near my house who requires ID with every debit card purchase. ID? You betcha! And finally, one never knows when a rapid exit to a third world country may be in order, to lay low until the heat blows over.

The notebook and pen are mandatory because I, by God's design, am blonde and I, by nature, am stupid. I receive flashes of brilliance in tiny increments that leave my head as quickly as they enter. So in order to utilize the random thoughts or inspirations that happen my way in later journaling, it becomes necessary for me to jot them down. Any type of writing I do requires me to refer back to notes and thoughts I document as they occur.

I always bring two books. I bring the one I am reading at the time of the trip and a back-up in case of completion of book #1, loss of book #1, or failure of book #1 to retain my attention. I can never be without something to read, especially in an airport or late at night in a hotel. The magazine is brought to give my mind a break from the book or books I'm reading. A mental recess if you will. Look, I never said any of this should make sense to you. I simply said this is what is in my pack and why I bring it.

The iPod and headphones are a necessity because music is, and always has been, a very important part of my life. The soundtrack for any given adventure must be carefully considered because the chosen songs will be tied to the memories created. You can't depart an airplane on a tropical runway with Mötley Crüe blaring from your ear buds, nor can you travel through a quiet Rocky Mountain morning with The Sex Pistols in your ear canals. Both are arguably great bands but should be called upon when appropriate. Music is a must and must be chosen with due diligence.

The phone charger is included because cell phones are as much a part of our daily lives as our lungs and every bit as vital. Very few things are as frustrating as having a low battery and no way to charge it. The charger must be kept close, just as close as the digital camera. With the camera, you can document your entire vacation and sort and edit the pictures on the go, limited only by the size of your memory card. I recommend having plenty of memory. Anyone who has reached the end of the camera memory card while on vacation or at an important event understands that size truly matters.

Finally, I carry gum and snacks. The gum is to fight the cranium splitting cabin pressure equalization problems during takeoff and landing, and the snacks are a necessity because no one wants to be hungry on an airplane. Everyone has experienced the twenty minute gap between the peanuts and the drink cart leading to dehydration and rapid consumption of the four ounce beverage placed on your tray. Once you have swallowed twice and taken in your entire allotment of soda, the remaining ice is then crunched and sucked until there is not an ounce of moisture left in the cup (I certainly may *not* have the ENTIRE can of Dr Pepper on my five hundred dollar flight. How gluttonous of me.). The right snacks can be consumed prior to boarding in order to curb the in-flight munchies, or they can be used for survival purposes during the "slight delay" on the runway.

My loaded green backpack, along with a large, black, canvas duffel containing kayak parts, and two smaller duffel bags completely packed with boating and camping supplies all sat idle near my front door, testing the holding strength of their respective zippers. That pile represented the past year of my life: my time, my money, my thoughts, my efforts, and even more of my money. I felt a certain satisfaction when I created the pile that night, yet self-defeating thoughts still entered my head as I offered myself consolatory congratulations: "Well, if nothing else, the boats were built, and I'll be in the Virgin Islands. I can at least say we made it that far."

Takeoff

The morning of October 8th I woke before the sun came up. I woke before my alarm clock sounded. I woke before I wanted to. That morning was different than any other departure morning. It was 4:00 a.m. and my mind was already racing as I mentally scrutinized the itinerary, reviewed mental checklists, and stressed over the remaining unanswered questions, such as "Will the boats go together correctly," "Will the boats float," "Will we survive?"

I'm fairly certain I brushed my teeth and put on my clothes that morning, but couldn't swear to anything. I may just as well have put toothpaste on the toilet brush, cleaned the bowl, and then dressed the dog. My mind had flushed the drama from the day before, along with the accompanying headache, and was completely occupied by what was about to happen. I could hear the clicks of the roller coaster car climbing the giant hill. The big drop was coming, and there was nothing I could do about it.

My wife was kind enough to get up at that painfully early hour and keep me focused enough to ensure the boat and my bags were packed into the trunk. I think at that point she just wanted me and the boat gone. Throughout the course of the previous year she had grown to loathe the word kayak. She, along with the other wives, had picked up the slack created by our countless hours in John's garage. While we toiled away at the boats, they took care of the kids; handling the homework, the baths, the skinned knees, the practices, the field trips, and everything else in real life that needed tending. We would not have made it to this point, heading to the airport with a trunk full of kayak if it were not for their patience and willingness to be the single parents for a while.

The streets were cold, dark, and empty as we drove to the airport in silence. The excitement of going to the Caribbean was the gasoline in my tank because, by all other accounts, I was completely exhausted. Plus, it was 4:30 in the morning and my body does not function well in the small hours. Even though it was too late to go back for anything at this point, I continued to obsess over and compare what would be needed for the trip with what I had packed, to ensure the lists matched.

At the airport I stepped away from the car and went directly to the baggage check booth. I dropped the two smaller duffels, leaned towards the boat bag, and lunged my body weight in the opposite direction, heaving it onto the counter. I don't know if it was the crash of the aluminum in the bag hitting the countertop that attracted so much attention or the awkwardly audible grunt I let fly when I tossed it up there. Either way, several handlers walked over to me with the combined look of curiosity and, "am I seriously going to have to lift that" on their faces. After answering a few questions about the bag and the trip, I offered my credit card up and with a little over a hundred dollars tacked onto my bill for the baggage, I strolled into Kansas City International Airport with both the literal and figurative weight lifted.

John, Eric, and I had made separate flight arrangements and were to meet in Miami, so I was making this flight alone. Because I was early for my flight, the airport was a ghost town. Had I been running late, the entire terminal would have looked like a *Where's Waldo* picture with no Waldo. As it was, I checked in, sailed through security, and grabbed a seat with two hours to kill until my flight. For the first time in a month I drew a deep breath, eased back into the extraordinarily uncomfortable airport chair, and allowed myself a moment of reflection. The entire process, from our first conversation about our idea to that moment at Gate 37, replayed in my mind. I would have preferred the memories to appear to me as an 80's movie style montage with the cheesy synthesizer pop song soundtrack, but instead they flashed through my mind as a slide show of random moments from the past year in no discernible order like the traumatic flashbacks of a war veteran, but completely different.

As the past year came and went through my cerebrum, the mental imagery shifted from what was behind me to what was ahead. It was a beautiful moment of surrender. I temporarily stopped caring if the boat would go together or if it would float. Sure, I wanted everything to go as planned and I did not want to return defeated to face everyone's questions about the trip, questions whose answers would inevitably be met with laughter and "I told you so's." But I had laid down the mental burden. There was nothing to do at this point except enjoy the ride. The hard work was done, and I was going to spend the next ten days in the Virgin Islands. *No worries, mon.* ("No worries, mon" was a common phrase uttered by John, in a poor Jamaican accent, prior to the trip. I constantly reminded him that we were NOT going to Jamaica. He didn't care. I knew he didn't care because he continually replied, "I don't care".)

I drew the magazine from my backpack and must have flipped from the front cover to the back and the back cover to the front three times before I realized that nothing was registering. My limited available mental space was filled with images of sand, palm trees, crystal clear water, and everything else waiting for me on the other side of the plane ride. I became incredibly restless as the time passed torturously slow. I switched positions in the airport seat about every thirty seconds, and I looked at my watch twice as often. I paced the floor like an expectant father. The dreary, overcast sky and scene of the lifeless concrete outside the terminal window increased my desire to leave it all behind. The dull grey of the skies obscured the sunrise and matched my general attitude about the Midwest at that moment.

Boarding the plane and finding my seat, I felt like a sprinter settling into the starting blocks. The flight crew closed the cabin door to the airplane as well as everything I was leaving behind in Kansas. I turned off my phone and iPod because I didn't want to be the one person who actually caused the plane to crash during take-off because I had failed to turn off my portable electronic equipment. Due to my thrifty airfare purchase, I received a good rate but had a dozen layovers at every city with a road straight enough that could be used as a landing strip between Kansas City and St. Thomas. My first layover was Dallas, Texas.

We touched down in Dallas to more grey skies, cold weather, and rain. That was not the way I was hoping to start the trip. During the brief layover something remarkable happened. The terminal was an atrium with a second story walkway. I was busy killing time perusing the gift shops deciding if I should buy the five dollar candy bar or the "Don't Mess with Texas" shot glass when I noticed a shift in the hustle and bustle of travelers. No one was sprinting or throwing hip checks to catch a departing plane. People were standing still and the terminal grew quiet. I took two steps out of the gift shop and saw everyone looking up. My gaze was drawn to the second story walkway where U.S. soldiers returning from an overseas deployment had exited their plane and were walking to meet their connecting flight. The terminal erupted in applause that did not weaken until the final soldier was out of sight. Thank you soldiers for what you do and thank you fellow travelers for joining me in a rare moment of overwhelming patriotism not felt since September 11, 2001.

Next stop – Miami. I had a long layover in Miami ahead of me but was looking forward to the rendezvous with Eric and John. Once we were all together I felt like the trip would officially be underway. I had not said a word to Eric since we parted ways at John's house the night before and was curious to see if our blowup at John's would carry over and affect the trip.

About the time I was choosing my seat for that leg of the flight, I realized that I had yet to outgrow my love of the window seat. I fly often and do everything in my power to secure the cherished seat next to the window. If there are no assigned seats and it is a first-come first-served airline, I am not above racing a child and tossing my backpack from four rows away into an open window seat in order to claim it. I was informed on one particular flight to Tampa, Florida that standard shotgun rules do not apply on an aircraft. Typically for an automobile, once the vehicle is in sight, "shotgun" can be called and the front passenger seat is then spoken for. En route to Tampa several years ago, I walked the center aisle scanning side to side. The seats were filling up fast when I spotted the last remaining available window seat. There was one elderly woman in front of me who could possibly plant her flag on my island. I did what any rational adult would do. I pointed and loudly (in a manner that could be taken as joking, even though I wasn't) said, "Dibs!" The woman in front of me turned to me, and in a dry tone, said, "Unless you can get around my fat ass in this narrow aisle, you might want to start looking for another seat." Well played ma'am. On that flight to Tampa I sat in a middle seat at the back of the plane between a snorer and a talker and contemplated which I would kill first or if it would just be easier to pull the vomit bag over my head and pray for the sweet embrace of death.

There is so much to hate about the act of commercial air travel: the belittling post 9/11 security checkpoints, the overpriced airport food and drinks, the crammed seating, the recycled air, the over talkers, snorers, one and a half seat takers, arm rest monopolizers, and the body odor. But to me, it's the bigger picture I dislike about flying. Flying isn't *traveling*, it is transporting. You aren't experiencing anything. You are doing your best, for a given period of time, to both ignore and be ignored until you get to point B.

Theroux wrote, "I dislike planes. And whenever I am in one - suffering the deafening drone and the chilly airlessness that is peculiar to planes - I always suspect that the land we are overflying is rich and wonderful and that I am missing it all." That is why I love the window seat. It's as close as I can get to experiencing anything other than the dull headache and time watching that comes with commercial air travel.

Flying into Miami I had secured the window seat. I have never had the patience to be able to meditate, but staring out the window of an aircraft is the closest I have ever been to achieving meditative enlightenment and a Zen like feeling. With my ear buds in place, I stare out into the vast expanse of the earth and its atmosphere. I often look down in amazement when I see how we humans have divided up the planet into squares and how we buy and sell those squares as if they are truly ours to begin with. Sunrise and sunsets from the window seats could rival those seen at the ocean or in the mountains. To me, the window seat is as much a part of the experience as most other parts of any trip, and certainly the best part of air travel.

Touching down in Miami I saw sunshine and palm trees. I smiled. I've often said that I know I'm where I want to be when I see palm trees. Palm trees, like me, do not fare well in cold climates. The warm greeting was just what I needed to start getting my mind right.

The Trio Reunited... Almost

Once the okay was given by the flight crew, I turned on my cell phone and was immediately greeted with a voicemail alert. I was still staring out the window at the sunshine and envisioning the three of us pushing off from a tropical beach in a glorious ruckus like cowboys in the old west riding out of town together. The voice message on my phone was from John: "Hey man. My flight out of Kansas City was cancelled. They are putting me on a later flight, and I can make it as far as Puerto Rico tonight. I should be in St. Thomas tomorrow and can meet you guys then. I checked my boat so have no idea if it will meet me in the islands or not. I'm headed to the nearest terminal bar. Call me." *Shit*.

I later found out that in Kansas City, John had boarded a plane headed for Miami and then the Virgin Islands. But, before takeoff the pilot had informed the passengers that they had a light bulb issue. He assured them there were no mechanical problems and that this would be resolved quickly. Thirty minutes later he was back on the intercom advising them that the light bulb issue was taking longer than expected, and they might possibly have to ground the flight. He said anyone wishing to deplane to make other arrangements could volunteer to do so at that time. John, seeing the writing on the wall, already had his carry-on bag in hand and was hurriedly "excuse me" and "pardon me" -ing his way past women and children to get off the plane. At the ticket counter, he was already booking his alternate flight when he noticed the stampede of passengers leaving his plane after learning that the flight was, in fact, grounded.

A burned out light bulb set a chain of events into motion that, without intent or apology, would alter our entire trip. We had no idea at the time how our itinerary would be modified by John's flight change. He caught another flight that took him to San Juan, Puerto Rico, and he would catch up with us the following day.

Eric was still on schedule and after I wasted a few hours in the Miami airport, he appeared. Because we hadn't spoken since the redneck verbal pissing contest in John's driveway the day before, I wasn't sure what to expect. With caution I offered a tentative, "hey." He laughed and asked, "Did you get the word about John?" Okay, the ice was broken. We chatted for a few minutes and then, since we still had about three more hours to kill, decided to find the nearest establishment serving adult beverages. We began to walk in search of a bar when he stopped. "Listen, I don't want an elephant in the room today or any other day of this trip. I was stressed and in a bad mood yesterday. I'm sorry." I offered a return apology, telling him that we would not be taking this trip if it weren't for him and that I had been juggling family and kayak as best I could and both had suffered. We threw a quick, one armed bro-hug, looked around to make sure no one had seen us, and the tension was gone. Brothers can fight like cats and dogs but at the end of the day, they are still brothers.

In the spirit of the trip, we drank Red Stripe beer in the airport bar as we looked at the charts and discussed our tentative itinerary. Yes, I know Red Stripe is Jamaican beer, but it was close enough. The beauty of the entire discussion was the optimism we maintained despite the frustration of our original plans. John was somewhere between KC and Puerto Rico. His boat was in a transit limbo, and we couldn't be positive when either of them were going to show up on St. Thomas. Yet, we devised plans A, B, and C. Plans A and B included three men and three boats exploring the islands. Plan C included three men, two boats, and one location where we would all stay and alternate taking day trips in the boats.

Eric and I flew from Miami to St. Thomas with very little conversation. We both quietly pondered the questions we had been avoiding: Have we bitten off more than we can chew? Would we be able to pull this off? With untested boats built by the three of us, having no boat building experience and zero ocean kayaking experience, were we adventurous or had we miscalculated our risks and naively inflated our own abilities?

This heavy thinking was interrupted only by my realization and shock that our in-flight movie was *Grease*. Yes, *Grease:* the musical that (not so) masterfully captured teenage angst and love and set it to song. You've heard the songs from *Grease* if you've ever found yourself at any karaoke bar on any night anywhere throughout the world. Karaoke, by the way, I believe is Japan's revenge on us for the whole atomic bomb thing. I could not believe that of all the possible movie options, we were graced with... *Grease*.

Touchdown in Paradise

Under the dark of night we touched down in Charlotte Amalie, St. Thomas. At Cyril E. King airport in Charlotte Amalie you exit the plane the old-fashioned way, by way of a roll up staircase. A few steps behind Eric, I felt the warm salty air greet my face as I crossed the threshold of the cabin door. I closed my eyes, inhaled as much tropical breeze as I could, and was happy. Sea breezes are a drug to which I am hopelessly addicted. We walked down the steps and onto the tarmac. The familiar hills to the north were speckled with the occasional house light. The stars were out in full force, and the temperature was around mid to upper perfect.

We collected our bags and after carrying them only a few steps towards the waiting taxi cabs, the reality of how heavy our boats actually were set in. We both made awkward smiles and light jokes about them, neither of us admitting that maybe we should have formulated a different plan for getting them to where the kayaking was to begin.

The taxi cabs in the Virgin Islands are comprised of vans and open air safaris (converted trucks with bench seating in the bed area). A nice benefit to utilizing Virgin Island cabs is that there is no haggling like in many parts of the Caribbean. The cabs are not metered. Prices are set by the government and listed as public information. Like polite vultures waiting for a meal, the cabbies were quietly lined up outside the airport waiting for the Americans to request their services and begin tossing tourist dollars their way.

I knew that the *Emerald Beach Hotel* was not far from the airport. When I told the cabbie where we wanted to go, he simply replied "yes," and began loading our bags. He heaved each boat bag into the back of the van but offered not so much as a strained look or a comment. Eric and I climbed in and were ready to be delivered to *Emerald Beach*. The cabbie got in, pulled the gear shifter into drive, and we pulled away from Cyril E. King airport. We drove for what seemed like about sixty yards when he pulled up to the front of the hotel, raised the shifter into park, said "Tirty dollas," and began to unload our bags.

Our large luggage caused our cab fare to climb to thirty dollars for a cab ride that covered the approximate distance that I could have punted a football. We didn't mind much and were able to laugh it off. We checked in and lugged our bags to our room. They seemed to have already doubled in weight, and we had to stop every ten steps or so to put the boat bags down and rest our fingers. That was going to be a problem, but first thing was first – the room.

We dropped the bags just inside the door. I entered, and without even asking if Eric had a preference, I claimed one of the beds by dropping my body weight onto it with the full force of my 185 pounds. We had made it! A wave of weary accomplishment rolled over me. If nothing else, we had built our boats and brought them to the Virgin Islands. It was one more incremental step towards the ultimate goal.

Despite the exhaustion from cramming to complete the boats, traveling all day on very little sleep, and dragging an overweight duffel bag full of a pipe dream, we weren't ready to turn in for the night. We were in the islands! From my previous visit I knew that when the sun goes down, most businesses close their doors. It was pushing 10:00 p.m. and was going to be difficult to find some place willing to feed us. Eric and I decided to head down to the beach bar/restaurant to try our luck.

As I suspected the lights of the open air restaurant were still on, but for no one in particular. There were no patrons. The only humans in sight were at the bar nestled in between the dining area and the sand. There was one bartender and one couple sitting at the bar. The bartender was obviously closing up shop. Eric and I wandered down to basically beg for a mercy meal and a drink. Anyone who has ever worked in the food service industry knows that you NEVER come in right before closing time to order food. Bad things happen. That was a risk we were willing to take.

We approached the bar and could feel the sideways look from the bartender. I politely asked if it was too late to get something to eat and a drink. He responded with "eeeeeeehhhhh, let me check with the kitchen," which is code for "are you kidding me?!?!" He checked with the kitchen staff and surprisingly came back telling us that they would make us each a burger but that would be it. Perfect! We'll take it! Now, about that drink. He had put most of the bottles away for the night but had in his hand a bottle of Pusser's rum. "I can make you something with this", he said holding up the bottle that sparkled like a diamond in the soft bar lights.

"Sold", I replied. "Anything will be fine".

He quickly dumped the rum into a shaker with a pre-mixed fruity concoction and poured our drinks. The addition of a few umbrellas completed the overpriced tourist cocktail ensemble. He set the cups down in front of us. "Pour us two more each and then you can stow the bottle and we'll pay our tab", I said. I think he was happy to find that we were not going to be keeping him any later than we already had.

The couple around the corner of the bar talked quietly to themselves and seemed oblivious to our presence. Eric and I touched our plastic cups together and toasted to two-thirds of us being in the islands. We didn't speak for several minutes, absorbing the warm, salty breeze and the soft sound of the waves rolling up on the sand, barely visible under the reflection of the moon and the stars.

Finally aware that they were not alone, the couple at the bar said hello. They asked if it was our first time in the islands, as if Eric and I were a couple. "Yeah," Eric said, "I was here a few years ago on my honeymoon. ...with my WIFE," he added to clear up any possible doubts.

"Don't you love it here?" the woman asked just as every other tourist asks when they encounter another tourist in the islands. She then followed up with the obligatory next question,

"Where are you guys from?"

"Kansas City."

Any time I travel and am asked where I'm from, I usually receive one of two responses. Immediately following "Kansas City," I hear "ahhhh…," followed by an awkward silence. It ends there. No one knows anything about Kansas City other than the fact that it is thoroughly unremarkable: they know not a single conversational fact about the climate, the sports teams, the architecture, the performing arts, or the non-existent night life. More often than not I hear my personal favorite, "Well, you're not in Kansas anymore." That quote from *The Wizard of Oz* along with the movie's depiction of Kansas as a wasteland of farmhouses, crops, and tornados sealed Kansas' fate as a glorious synonym for nothingness.

The man and woman opted for the much appreciated evasion of it altogether and replied, "We're from Illinois." The following half hour, as I write this, is a blur. Even discussing it with Eric months after the trip, neither of us could recall the specific details of the bar conversation that night. Basically it was the man talking incessantly and the woman sprinkling in support and affirmation in the form of "mmhhmm" and "yep." He rambled something about his stint at an Iowa auctioneering college and how his family called an intervention to confront him about his "shit-all wrong" bi-polar diagnosis. Then, either they sent him, or he voluntarily went to the Mayo Clinic where, to prove he wasn't crazy or bipolar, he rolled through an example of his auctioneering skills to the doctor and said, "Could a crazy man do that?" He obviously proved his point to the doctor who allowed him to return to Illinois, victorious, with a clean bill of health and a renewed confidence in his ability to yell numbers in an organized fashion really quickly.

After our escape from the mayo clinic rebel/part time auctioneer and his significant other, Eric and I headed down from the bar and walked the twenty feet or so down to the water for a close up look at the ocean. It was getting late and with our bellies full and a couple of rum drinks down, it was time to call it a night. We recapped the previous conversation with the couple we had met at the bar and confessed it was for just those reasons we both love the islands; strangers are not strangers and everyone has a story. After about ten minutes of conversation it dawned on both of us that we were a couple of dudes taking a slightly buzzed, romantic moonlight stroll along the beach. We both laughed but not for long. We quickly turned back towards the hotel and talked of manly things to recapture some semblance of our straightness and began a humorous discourse of why we both only eat popsicles sideways.

Once back in the room we organized our bags in hopeful anticipation of John and his boat arriving early the next day, allowing us to pull the trigger on the adventure. The room was silent but our heads were filled with clutter wondering what was to come. I quietly said a quick prayer thanking God for the opportunity to be in the Virgin Islands and for the opportunity to see just how close He and I were going to get in the following week. I had a feeling I would be talking and negotiating with the Man upstairs many times in the days to come. I reached up and turned the light off in the room and on the day. We had made it.

CHAPTER 4

The Plan (Almost) Comes Together

I woke around 9:00 a.m. to the faint glow of tropical sunlight creeping through the cracks in the curtain and the soothing sound of the waves lapping up on the shore. Actually the waves didn't sound soothing at all. They sounded like an angry, buzzing fly trying to escape through a window. As I lifted my confused brain from the bacterial breeding ground, otherwise known as the hotel pillow, it occurred to me that the angry fly was my cell phone buzzing and dancing on the night stand. It was John. He had arrived on St. Thomas and, of course, his boat had not. Fortunately, he had been told that it was en route and should arrive on the 3:00 p.m. flight into Charlotte Amalie. John asked for our room number as he climbed into a cab for the ninety second ride to the hotel.

Eric woke up during my phone call with John and picked up enough from my half of the conversation to figure out what was going on. We were both relieved that John was on the island and the boat was at least *supposed* to be on its way as well. I sat up and traversed the tile floor to the sliding glass door. I pulled the curtains open to reveal a sunny, cloudless day and, beyond the palm tree growing within arm's reach of our balcony, was the water I had been dreaming about. Regardless of what hand fate was going to deal us that day, the morning had started off the way I needed it to – beautifully and slowly.

A few minutes later, there was a knock at the door. John walked in with simply the clothes on his back and a smile. "Do we have to put the damn boats together or can we just tell people we did and hang out here on the beach instead? I could get used to this place!" He had been on the island for less than an hour and had already adapted and fallen in love with the climate and the lifestyle. Island life is not for everyone and certainly takes an adjustment. Nearly all of us live in the fast lane. We eat drive-thru dinners in our car, we get angry if we have to wait in line at Wal-Mart for more than a minute, and if our internet connection takes longer than four seconds to load a page, our day is simply ruined. Our lives have become so dependent on technology and so accelerated that adjusting to a simpler lifestyle, where everyone is not in a hurry, can be maddening. Try going to a shop on St. Anywhere in the Caribbean and ask them what time they close. A typical response is, "I don't know, five or six. Maybe four." For us mainlanders it is unfathomable to run a business that opens and closes whenever it wants to. If the shopkeeper has a good morning, he may close up at lunch time and go next door to the bar for the remainder of the day. It seems they are driven by money, but not controlled by it. A day or two may pass before one realizes it is we who have the problem and not them. Once that bolt of lightning strikes you, life becomes much easier in the islands. As John would and often did say, "No worries, mon".

Since the boat would not arrive until three, we had several hours to kill and decided to head into downtown Charlotte Amalie to spend some time and money. The bustling capital of the U.S. Virgin Islands was named for Charlotte Amalie of Hesse-Kassel, who, through an arranged marriage, became queen consort to King Christian V of Denmark. He ruled in the late 1600s to early 1700s and was a busy man, fathering eight children with his wife and five with mistresses. Through it all Charlotte Amalie remained a class act and earned the love and respect of many, which is why, after the Dutch conquered St. Thomas in 1666, the capital was eventually named for her.

The population of Charlotte Amalie is typically around 20,000 people give or take. That number swells each time a big white cruise ship eases into port. It is the most popular tourist spot in the Virgin Islands, hosting between one and two million cruise ship visitors per year. The downtown area is filled with a plethora of shops eager to offer cruisers that perfect souvenir. Eric, John, and I weren't after any souvenirs just yet, but we did want to pick up a few odds and ends.

Cassius and Gladys

The three of us strolled out of the front of the hotel and hopped into the one cab that sat alone in the circle drive. If you've never been to the Virgin Islands, I will let you in on a little secret. There are a variety of things to do on the island as well as in, on, and under the water; but the real adventures happen in the cabs. The drivers are almost always full of personality and advice. They have mastered the mathematical equation of personalized cab ride = good tip. Most of the drivers I've encountered in the little latitudes are transplants from smaller islands who relocate in order to cash in on the Caribbean's most valuable commodity: American dollars. Our cab ride into Charlotte Amalie came courtesy of Cassius.

Cassius appeared to be in his mid- fifties. He had the energy of a teenager and the wisdom of the ancients. He also happened to be a basketball fan. More specifically, he was a University of Kansas basketball fan. He and John, a KU alum, connected immediately, talking of past and present players. It was interesting to witness the conversation between John and this St.

Thomas cabbie, who had left the island only a handful of times in his life. They talked as if they were neighbors at the local sports bar rather than strangers in a minivan cruising along tiny island roads.

At one point Cassius shifted gears from roundball to dispensing advice on life and love. He had been married for many years and reared several island kids, fancying himself somewhat of a seasoned philosophical man. Cassius had a mantra: "Life is an attitude, OK buddy?" He offered it to us, tagging on the end a half-hearted request for affirmation. Okay, granted, his statement was not necessarily profound, yet somehow, coming from this island sage, it seemed deep to us. We squinted our eyes and with protruded bottom lips nodded to each other in approval as if he had unlocked the long lost secret to happiness.

We drove into the heart of downtown Charlotte Amalie. The port area was predominantly 18th century masonry warehouses that were converted into duty free shops and wrapped in pretty, warm, pastel colors. I was relieved to see that no ships were in port that morning so the downtown area was operating, but not necessarily bustling. I mentioned to Cassius that I was glad to see that we would not be battling big crowds. He replied, "Everyone in da square dis mornin. Da new kwata come out." Eric and I looked at each other hoping the other knew what in the hell a "kwata" was. John, having somewhat made sense of what he said asked, "The new quarter?" "Yes, da Virgin Island kwata."

OH! Okay. Starting in 1999 the U.S. Mint started giving each state their own quarter; they must have finished the fifty states and had some extra material around so gave the U.S. territories some monetary recognition. I was still processing the "new kwatas" when we slowed to a stop due to downtown traffic. I looked to my right to see the Caribbean ocean. It was vast, blue-green, and sparkling; and it was calling. Cassius broke my trance by pointing to his left. "If you want good place to eat, you go to *Gladys'*. Mmmm. You will like! Tell them Cassius sent you and they fix you up." Which translates to, "Gladys is my wife, sister, or friend, and I get a kickback if you mention my name."

We parted ways with Cassius and wandered into the main square where hundreds of locals had gathered to wait in line for their free Virgin Islands "kwata." The three of us milled around for a few minutes and quickly decided that we should skip the souvenir quarters and pick up some necessities like sun block and beer. We performed our obligatory tourist walk through the market and opted to pass on their wares which consisted of anything and everything that could possibly labeled "St. Thomas" or "Virgin Islands," all made in China, of course.

Despite my skepticism about the intentions of Cassius' advice, we decided to give *Gladys'* a shot. We were in the islands and, even if there was one, we sure as hell weren't going to sit at a Taco Bell. *Gladys'* was not on the main drag with a big marquee sign and outside seating so the tourists feel more tropical as they eat their "authentic" island food and insanely overpriced drinks. You have to walk through an alley to find *Gladys'*. I have learned going to places with an alley-only entrance goes one of two ways; it will either be a colossal mistake and you will end up in front of a police officer, a doctor, or both; or it will be the coolest fucking place you have ever been. We walked into *Gladys'* and it was exactly what I hoped. It was a little bit dirty yet inviting. There were three or four black women waiting tables who completely ignored us. Seated at one table was a couple in their fifties who were obviously tourists and must have been Cassius's last fare. Other than the pasty couple in the St. Thomas t-shirts, every patron looked as if they belonged there. They were as much a part of the atmosphere as the blue and white checkered plastic tablecloths and the framed pictures hanging crooked on the antique rock and brick walls.

"Tree of you?" A woman with a worn but friendly face was quickly approaching from behind us.

"Yes, please."

"Dis way," she said with the biggest smile I had seen in a long time. With fine precision she set down three menus and just as many glasses of water with varying degrees of questionable clarity. "She be right wit you," she informed us while never breaking stride as she moved towards the kitchen. "She" showed up right away and took our drink orders. In fine tourist fashion, we ordered the fruitiest rum drinks we could find on the one page laminated menu, and each opted to try the special: curry chicken with peas and rice, plantains, and a sweet potato.

The drinks arrived first and within minutes lunch was served. The meal looked... well... yellow. Everything on the plate was a similar shade of baby excrement. The peas and rice were formed into a yellow baby excrement bell shape that rose about four inches above the plate. The yellow baby excrement plantains and sweet potato lay in a pool of yellow baby excrement fluid, which surrounded the yellow baby excrement chicken. I picked up my fork, and with a look of part disgust and part curiosity, I began to poke the chicken like a child would poke a dead bird with a stick. Eric was the first to laugh out loud. John and I immediately followed.

The flavor was surprisingly good but slightly bland. Sitting in the middle of the table, in the same glass pint bottles you would see behind the counter at the liquor store, were several offerings of homemade hot sauce. Not one of the options displayed a heat rating or parental warning label. John and I decided to spice the meal up a bit and sample some local flavor with our local dish. The first sauce was tangy and had a little bit of a bite. In unison we nodded and shoulder shrugged as the universal sign of "ehhh... not bad." It was time for hot sauce number two. I poured a small puddle on an outer edge unoccupied portion of my plate. Somehow this stuff permeated everything on my plate like a bad horror movie. One of God's cruel jokes is the time it takes for extremely spicy food to register in your brain. There is a rise in temperature that takes about ten seconds to register that a corrosive material has entered your mouth and is currently dissolving your taste buds and tooth enamel.

By bite number three John and I were drinking entire glasses of water in a single gulp and wiping sweat, snot, and possibly blood from most of our facial orifices. One waitress walked by and noticed two grown men who were crying and repeatedly and rhetorically asking, "Why? Why-hi?" She had obviously seen that reaction before and said, "Oh yes, Gladys makes a MAD hot sauce!" I sarcastically replied, "No kidding?!?" Actually I tried to say that, but all she heard were whimpers that were gurgling through a bloody pharynx and reverberating off newly formed oral burn blisters.

We crawled sniffling out of *Gladys'*, and decided to recover at our hotel beach until John's boat arrived. A short cab ride and a quick wardrobe change later, we were sitting in the sand drinking cold beer. The sun was high in the sky and heat felt good against my spf 15 covered skin. The salty air was invigorating. Well, the salty air was invigorating to ME. We had only been on the beach about ten minutes when Eric fell asleep in a beach chair. The poor guy was still exhausted from the past forty eight hours. John wandered out into the water to cool off. I closed my eyes for a few moments of tropical mediation and then did what I always do. I got up and went exploring.

I don't know if it's the kid in me, the undiagnosed ADHD, or an underlying boredom phobia, but when I am in a new place I have a hard time sitting still. I want to explore! I would say most people spend their entire year stressing about bills and kids and marriage and divorce and cocktail parties and time lines and deadlines, and everything else that creates our self-imposed life clutter. Many of those people will take four or five days out of that year and book themselves a tropical vacation where they can relax, take in the scenery, catch a buzz and a sunburn, and untangle their mental bird's nests. I, on the other hand, cannot just lay on the beach and watch the tide roll in and out. I want to know what's out there.

So while Eric anchored down the beach chair and John cooled off in the surf, I grabbed my snorkel and mask and headed out to explore the reef that lined the eastern edge of Emerald Bay. I spent nearly an hour swimming back and forth over the reef where it must have been break time because the view was thoroughly uneventful. The one exception was a wayward turtle whom I followed and clearly annoyed because I inadvertently drove him away from a potential reef snack.

Time to Leave the Country

Three o'clock came quickly and it was time for the adventure to begin. We gathered our things and met our old friend Cassius in front of the hotel. He was right on time and happy to see us. I don't think he was pleased so much by the three cool guys from America as much as his guaranteed fare. Regardless, he greeted us with a warm smile that disappeared when he began loading our mountainous pile of kayak-in-a-bag bags and accompanying luggage into his cab for our trip to the airport and then the ferry dock.

We pulled into the airport where John and Eric scurried inside to retrieve John's kayak. I remained in the cab with Cassius and listened to him once again enlighten me with his discourse about life, family, and the pursuit of happiness. I was so eager to get the third boat and get started on our adventures that I gave Cassius the same attention I gave my grandfather when he used to talk about growing up on a Missouri farm or World War II – virtually none. However, as with my grandfather, I now regret not being more attentive. They both freely offered wisdom that I was too preoccupied to appreciate. Within a few minutes, Eric and John emerged from the open air baggage claim, each with one end of John's kayak bag in his hand. I didn't realize until that moment how much I needed visual confirmation that the third boat had really arrived. Once I saw that hefty black canvas bag swinging between them, I felt a wave of relief sweep over me and my subconscious stress level dropped by a factor of ten.

With well-timed dual grunts, they heaved John's boat into the back of the cab. We pulled away, and Cassius gave a sharp swerve to the left planting my face against the right window. Not one to miss an opportunity to inflate his tip, he drove us alongside two newly arriving scantily clad women and offered to give them a ride as well. They smiled as they declined. Cassius pulled away and laughingly said, "I tried." Truthfully we were relieved. At that point we were focused and just wanted to get to the ferry dock so we could make our way to the British Virgin Islands (BVI).

Like the U.S.Virgin Islands, their British neighbors are comprised of a few major islands and a smattering of other smaller islands and cays. Depending on who you ask, there are as many as fifty British islands sprinkled just east of their U.S. counterparts. The four major islands are Tortola, Virgin Gorda, Anegada, and Jost Van Dyke. Tortola, which is the largest and contains the vast majority of the citizens of the BVI, was our original destination. Once checked in to the country, another ferry would take us the rest of the way to Virgin Gorda where we would begin our quest.

The Red Hook ferry dock was buzzing with locals who were waiting to catch a boat to one of the other islands. Most of them looked as if their shift on St. Thomas had ended or their shopping trip was done, and they were returning home. They barely noticed the three white guys who had exited Cassius' cab and were unloading enough sizeable bags to look like we were moving in. The golden walls and bright green roof of the terminal were a warm and welcome sight. It represented our gateway.

At the counter we requested our tickets to Tortola where we could check into the British islands. The kind woman behind the counter issued us each a one way ticket from Red Hook, St. Thomas to Roadtown, Tortola. It was about the time she began asking about our luggage that there was a change in the tone of our interaction. Any bags over fifty pounds were subject to additional per pound fees. Our bags were considerably over fifty pounds. I did not get to see the weight of the first bag on the scale, but the look on her face told me that if she was being paid on commission, her mortgage payment was covered for the month. Fortunately for us, another woman who was presumably the supervisor happened to be walking behind her and saw the number on the digital readout. She looked up and asked what was in the bag. When we told her the story, she was merciful enough to only charge us a nominal flat fee, which she likely put in her pocket because, in hindsight, she was just passing by and never entered any numbers into the cash register.

When the ferry boat arrived, we climbed aboard and watched as the dock workers strain against gravity and career ending hernias loading our bags. The ferry boat had all the class of an inner city bus. It was gritty but that only added to the ambience of the ride. We walked to the back, grabbed a few window seats, and plotted the rest of our day. As the ferry pulled away from the dock, the sun had already peaked and was in the process of its decent into the ocean. We were behind schedule and we were forced to alter our plans. Our initial goal to make Virgin Gorda by nightfall was no longer realistic, and we knew it. There simply weren't enough hours left in the day. Maps were pulled from our packs and the contingency plan was developed.

Once we cleared Customs and Immigration, we would only have a few hours of daylight left. From our research we knew there was a campground on the northern coast of Tortola at Brewer's Bay. The decision was made to set up camp and spend the night there. In the morning we could put the kayaks together and, depending on the weather, the topography, our instinct, or a coin toss, decide which direction to paddle.

Clearing Customs

I think I've already established that Eric had researched this venture down to the smallest details. In order to clear customs with our kayaks Eric had found that certain items would be required. Each kayak would have to be officially registered with a hull ID number as well as contain numerous mandatory safety items. We were not going to make it that far and be stopped by a customs agent that we would have to bribe. Prior to packing in Kansas City, we ensured that we had every item on the list and would not be denied based on a technicality.

We lined up with the rest of the ferry passengers and blazed through the process at a snail's pace. I was the first of the three to have to attempt getting a giant duffel bag full of kayak parts cleared. I was prepared to arrogantly respond to each of his requirement inquiries. I had spent the money and I had every single item on their list. The small black man who was wearing a short sleeved military shirt that looked like it belonged to his big brother asked,

"What's in de bag?"

"A kayak", I volleyed back and took a *bring it on* posture.

"OK," he said and waved me through.

OK? That's it?! Just OK?! I had made extra shopping trips and swiped my credit card to the point of transparency to make sure we met all Customs' requirements and all the official gave me was an OK! Prior to walking into the Customs building, I had envisioned a stone faced, square jawed military immigration specialist , looking at me through mirrored sunglasses, and rattling off item after item on his "Required For Entry" list in a thick Russian accent (I'm a cold war kid – all the bad guys have Russian accents even if we were in the British Virgin Islands.). With a few slight trickles of sweat cascading down my forehead, I would point out each item that he was naming. And finally, for his closing move, he would mutter in a very Dolf Lundgren (Rocky IV) voice, "Hull registration number," drawing it out very slowly and dramatically. I would close my eyes and drop my head in slow motion false defeat. The smile would start to creep slowly across his face. He wouldn't notice my left hand easing into my front pocket. I would pull out the folded registration form and slam it on the desk at which the rest of the tourists waiting in line would erupt into applause. Even the two guards in the corner, who secretly hated the British customs guy with the Russian accent, would look at each other and exchange slight and subtle smiles. I would strut through with an ego induced grin, high fiving random people.

Instead, the diminutive customs agent simply said, "OK," and waved me through. The baggage handler tossed my boat bag onto the floor and reached for the next piece of luggage. They never even opened the bag! I could have been smuggling in black market Nikes stuffed with pounds of heroin and foreign fruit. I was offended, but not for long. Eric and John passed through with equal ease, and we were officially on British soil.

To Brewer's Bay

As expected the cabbies were waiting outside the door. We, again, crammed our bags into the back of an island cab and headed north towards Brewer's Bay. The driver informed us there was a market in the middle of the island where we could stop and pick up the water and food we would need. We rambled along into the heart of Tortola, passing small coveys of locals who were smoking and drinking alongside the narrow road. The common theme among the groups was the laughing and smiling faces. They all appeared to be having a great time. It felt like we were passing an adult playground on a permanent recess.

With no discernible traffic right of way laws, the cabbie hit fourth gear on the winding road as the small concrete and sheet metal houses passed us in a blur. He honked the horn at every corner as a courtesy to any other driver or unsuspecting pedestrian who happened to be around the bend and in the cab's trajectory.

With dusk quickly approaching, we pulled into the market. This was our last known opportunity to pick up food and water, and we needed to stock up. There was about a one-chicken-to-five-person ratio wandering in and out of the grocery store. In front of the store there were stacks of cardboard boxes where jugs of milk were being handed out to Tortola natives. John and I climbed out of the sardine can minivan cab and wandered in. Eric stayed in the cab to keep an eye on our bags and ensure the cab didn't disappear along with everything we had. He tried in vain to make small talk, but the anti-Cassius cab driver seem more than mildly irritated to be transporting us that evening.

John and I meandered through the store grabbing anything we could think of that was non-perishable and/or life sustaining. We purchased in triplicate. We were not survivalists accumulating vacuum packed and freeze dried rations. We were shopping on pure impulse and paying little or no attention to cost. We were drunk with enthusiasm and shopped like a pair of twelve year olds with mom's credit card. There was no rhyme nor reason to our selections. Three loaves of bread, three jars of peanut butter, three cans of Vienna sausages, three boxes of Pop Tarts, three cans of Spaghettio's, three bags of chips, three bags of M&M's, six cans of Spam, six cans of tuna, six jugs of water, and three bottles of Cruzan rum, among other things, were piled into the small shopping cart.

We pushed our wheeled pack mule to the front of the store where the cashier began ringing up the contents of our pile without ever looking up. She located each price tag and typed the amounts into the circa 1960 cash register with what we hoped was some degree of accuracy. The grand total came to just a shade under $250. ...for groceries. ...for three men. ...for five or six days. I would estimate the same groceries at a local Kansas City market would have come in somewhere around eighty dollars. But we were in the middle of an island in the middle of the Caribbean and happy to be there. A quick swipe of the credit card, and we were cramming our plastic grocery sacks into the already overfull taxi cab.

The remainder of the drive north was a series of sharp turns and ups and downs. With each ascent our cabbie would downshift and the cab would slow in opposite proportion to the engine rpm's as it strained to climb. The motor wrapped up and screamed as we crept forward and watched pedestrians walk past us as if we weren't even there. After reaching the summit of each hill, the descent began and the driver would again down shift, testing the limits of the engine as it roared in defiance. Eric, John, and I began to see the potential fortune that could be made by a good transmission mechanic on the island of Tortola.

Under a blanket of darkness, we pulled into Brewer's Bay Campground. If there was a sign announcing it, we certainly couldn't see it. It was a little known campground and, being the off-season, signs of life were sparse. In hindsight the cab driver could have been delivering us to an encampment of machine gun toting drug lords who were going to kidnap us and sell us into black market sex slavery. No such luck, it was simply a dark tropical campground.

Campground Carl

We parked under the lone working streetlight. As if on cue and in the style of a bad horror movie, an ominous figure began to emerge from the shadows, slowly and unnervingly. An odd sound could be heard, but we couldn't quite tell what it was. Nervously, we paused from unpacking our bags to see what was approaching. Into the light inched Carl. Carl was apparently the proprietor of the campground and was a unique and unknowingly comical character. He was utterly listless and shuffled along at the speed of a stoned slug. He mumbled things under his breath that were barely audible above the small rectangle radio he carried that maintained a steady volume of eleven. The cab driver told him why we were there and what we needed, and Carl simply nodded in approval and waved us toward him.

Amidst a small mountain of kayak, duffel, and grocery bags, we opted to follow Carl and scope out the camp sites before hauling in. We walked at a quarter speed following Carl into the darkness. The only sounds were a rambling talk radio host blaring out of the tiny speaker of Carl's radio and the faint crash of waves hitting an unseen shore.

The path led us straight to the ocean. Carl pointed to the west towards the campsites and asked how long we would be staying. Eric, ever respectful, answered,

"One or two nights, sir."

"You can just pay before you leave," Carl mumbled as he turned and shuffled back to his home in the dark abyss. The sound of the radio disappeared with him and left us with the soft ocean breeze, a clear starry sky, and the sea.

The first thing Eric did was check-in, using the GPS device he had purchased prior to the trip. Building the boats was his idea, and he felt somewhat responsible for them, so he had brought along a backup plan. It was a small orange plastic rectangular box. With the push of a button, a predetermined message was sent to family members letting them know that we were OK. The message even listed our coordinates with which, if so inclined, they could look up our location. There was also an "oh shit" button. I'm sure it had a more proper name, but if things went really wrong, Eric could hit the "oh shit" button and the Coast Guard would be notified of our location and need for assistance. I made fun of it, but I was certainly glad that little insurance policy was always within reach.

I flipped on my flashlight and we investigated the campsites. Because of the darkness it was difficult to tell if there were any other campers. And when I say "campsites" don't assume that we were in a typical state park style campsite where there is a small gravel drive for a camper, a picnic table, and a fire pit. Paralleling the water were, from what we could tell, about six "sites." They consisted of pre-erected tents protected by tarp canopies which were held over the tents by weathered 2x4s nailed together. For a brief moment we considered the good fortune of having tents already in place which would save us the trouble of unpacking and repacking ours.

Without the benefit of knowing if anyone was there or not, we cautiously chose a site. We had to be sure we weren't moving in on someone else's territory, so I tossed the flashlight to John and said he should check inside the tent. Just as in cliché family vacation movies, in which a family arrives at their campsite to a myriad of offensive sights and smells, John opened the tent to a Petri dish of undiscovered parasite vitality waiting for three carrier monkeys to burrow into them. There were two mattress covered cots which were stained by any of variety of human or zoological fluids: sweat, slobber, piss, semen, and blood among others. Without saying a word, John removed his head, zipped the tent closed and simply said, "No."

The three of us made several trips back and forth between our mountain of bags and the campsite. Once everything was brought down to the shore campsite, we unpacked the groceries and divided them equally into three piles. With controlled eagerness we respectively set up our tents. John, the envy of Eric and me, had a bivy which was basically a netted body cover that, in theory, would allow wind in but not bugs. It did not leave much for privacy, but after living together in the firehouse for many years, there's not much left that we haven't seen and don't know about each other. Eric and I had backpacking tents, mine being the slightly larger of the two. We awkwardly positioned and repositioned flashlights in our teeth, in the sand, and in nearby bushes in an effort to illuminate the tent erection. The only noticeable sound was Eric, every few minutes asking, "Hey, has anybody seen my___." Fill in the blank with whatever camping or kayaking item you wish. It was likely mentioned. His misplacement of things and unorganized packing was comical. Within minutes there were three small imported tents huddled in front of the large, pre-erected, science experiment of a tent. I grabbed a twin pack of Pop Tarts for dinner and walked the surrounding area collecting dead palm branches for a fire.

To finish off our first official night removed from civilization, we walked away from the tents and campfire and found three plastic chairs by a nearby tent and dragged them down where the waves were rolling up on the sand. We sat in our swimming trunks and flip flops under an umbrella of a thousand stars and toasted our accomplishment. We had made a plan. We had struggled, sweat, laughed, fought, cussed, and ultimately constructed the boats. Although not yet together, they were sitting in bags in the sand on the beach of Tortola in the British Virgin Islands.

For our first toast, I told the story of a welder from New Jersey who I had met on the shore of St. Thomas several years before. He and I had chatted for a while as his wife and daughters played in the sand just beyond the reach of the water. He had made me laugh when he called me "Kansas" with his thick Jersey accent. ("You got any kids, Kansas?") Ready to call it a night, the family stood up and just stared out at the water for a minute. We all stared. We were joined in a tropical trance. He broke the silence, slapped me on the shoulder, and said, "Who's better 'n us tonight, right?"

"Who's better than us tonight?" I declared, and John and Eric laughed. We tapped our Cruzan rum bottles together and drank.

The rum was warm and sweet and tasted like victory! We raised a toast to Keith who could not be with us, but without whose help we would not have been there ourselves. Toast after toast was made. We drank rum from the bottle, questioned why we lived in Kansas, and relished our memories of the metaphoric mountains we had climbed to make it to this beach and begin our real journey. No matter what happened the next day, we had made it this far!

CHAPTER 5

Going Nowhere

Whoosh...Whoosh... Clang... Whoosh...Whoosh... Clang. Mumble. Mumble.

My eyelids parted to tepid light filtering through the palm trees and into my tent. I lay motionless for a few minutes appreciating the soothing sound of the waves and the way the sand beneath me had contoured to my body lending itself to a perfect night's sleep. I didn't remember falling asleep the night before when, with a moderate rum buzz, I climbed into my tent, wrote in my journal (man-diary), and lowered my head onto a small airplane pillow that I... ahem, *borrowed* on my flight down. The firm aggregate ground beneath my tent was not enough to prevent me from falling into a deep sleep. I slept very well and enjoyed the sound of the ocean and the full moon as my night light.

Clang. Clang. Whoosh. The familiar ringing of aircraft aluminum banging together interrupted the hypnotic monotony of the waves hitting the shore. Without looking, I knew that Eric was already at work unpacking his kayak parts from their bag. I drew a deep breath and sat up in my tent. My body resisted gravity with everything it had, but I made it to the seated position anyway. I felt good, foggy, but good. I unzipped my tent, poked my head out, and, through squinted eyes, saw Brewer's Bay for the first time. The lush green hills seemed to hug the moderately peaceful waters of the bay. The west side of the inlet dropped off at a steep rocky cliff while the east side angled gently into the sea. The wide mouth of the bay opened up revealing nothing but ocean as far as my half opened eyes could see. John was standing waist deep in the turquoise water giving himself a makeshift Caribbean camping bath while Eric knelt in the sand putting together his kayak. A side effect of my coma-like sleep was my complete inability to place time of day. For all I knew Eric might have actually been taking his kayak apart, and I had slept through the entire trip. The soft light illuminating the hills told me the sun was not very high in the sky and it had to be fairly early. In my morning fog it occurred to me that on my wrist was a marvel of modern technology that would tell me the time anytime I cared to look at it. According to my watch it was 6:24 a.m.

I stepped out of my tent with rubbery legs that felt foreign beneath me. I was awkward and graceless. The first few steps were almost painful as my body was in motion against its will. A pair of mismatched chickens meandered around the tents looking for, I assume, Pop Tart fallout from the night before. Looking down at them, I ordered a large coffee with two sugars and a vanilla scone, but the chickens continued to peck at the sand randomly and pretended not to hear me. They heard me. I reached for my bag of trail mix that our friend Stacy had made for each of us to take with us, and I grabbed a handful of breakfast. I sauntered down to the sand and sat on a small rock wall in silence.

Forced Perspective

Shadows enveloped most of the bay. I eased into a hypnotic suspension of lethargic philosophy. I thought of how many days I find myself sitting in a coffee shop sipping on the designer stimulant of the day. I surround myself with people buried in laptops and tablets who multitask conversation with smart phone navigation. Even with the full realization that I was one of them, I became disgusted with the human race. We don't engage, we interface. We get our political opinions from talk radio and our news in short, rapid-fire blasts due to our inability to give anything our attention for more than fifteen seconds. Society not only accepts, but encourages this. We are *supposed* to have a Bluetooth. We are *supposed* to know what a wifi hotspot is. We are *supposed* to be able to work, shop, and maintain relationships by way of a touch screen.

It is forced perspective. Forced perspective is a technique that uses distance as an optical illusion to create the impression that an object is closer, further, bigger, smaller, etc. than it actually is. This is very popular in photography and film making. Remember the picture of your friends who came back from Europe with pictures of themselves posing two blocks in front of the Leaning Tower of Pisa yet appear as if they are holding it up? That's forced perspective. We've all fallen victim to it and many times don't realize it.

Objects may be closer than they appear. Or in this case, objects may be further than they appear. Technology gives us the illusion of proximity. This is a huge disservice to us all and serves to hurt more than help in some cases. Everything is accelerated. If we don't get what we want or see what we want or hear what we want right now, we are disappointed or angry when not too long ago we were thrilled to get a letter in the mail from a distant friend or relative. Forced perspective has become so much a part of our every day that it is the standard. That morning on the beach, I did what every person does when they find themselves removed from real life and consider with abhorrence what they have become; I vowed to make a change. I would appreciate the little things. I would slow down. I would leave my cell phone behind. I would interact more face to face. I made all of those commitments with the full realization that my determination to simplify my life would fade in proportion with my tropical tan, and I would be back to my normal pasty white, hurried, impersonal lifestyle within weeks. I have been down that "change my ways" path many times, and I understand the process.

The Sweat Coffin and Kayak Construction

My reflections on the current state of the human condition were interrupted by John emerging from the water. Knowing his history of back pain issues I baited him.

"How'd you sleep last night?"

"I might have slept fine if I wasn't in a goddamn sweat coffin. If I have another night like that: hot, loud, and uncomfortable... fuck it, I'm getting a hotel".

John's bivy tent, which is made entirely of netting, had somehow defied the tropical trade winds and left John to broil in a "sweat coffin" while attempting to sleep. He would unzip the bivy to allow in a breeze which was accompanied by blood seeking bugs. He then zipped the tent back up to prevent more bugs from coming in and began to once again sweat, starting a vicious cycle which apparently lasted the majority of the night. At one point Eric said he woke to John's grumblings, stuck his head out, and saw John dragging a chair back down to the beach, effectively throwing in the towel in his battle to find sleep. Beyond John's mild grumbling, no one had any complaints. I think we all truly appreciated that we were basically alone on the shore of an amazingly scenic beach in the middle of the British Virgin Islands.

Eric was focused and already had his kayak out of its bag and placed in organized piles. He had yet to acknowledge me, but I knew Eric, and I knew he had spent the night tossing and turning wondering if the kayaks were going to come together and if they would indeed manage the salty swells waiting for us. Admittedly I was anxious to find out for myself. Within minutes the sand of Brewer's Bay was littered with piles of aircraft aluminum and three gringos working in hopeful silence, trying to piece together untested kayaks, except for the occasional call out from Eric, "Hey, has anybody seen my ___" that echoed across the beach.

The assembly went surprisingly smooth. The lengths were joined and bolted together at either end creating the familiar bow of the vessels. It took longer than I had anticipated, but we were on island time and did not once wonder about how slowly or quickly they were coming together; we simply *assembled*.

The bay, for the most part, was deserted. One particular passerby asked early on in construction what we were building. We told him our intentions, and he gave a perplexed and almost sympathetic smile. He wished us luck and walked away (He might at least have had the courtesy to get out of earshot before he giggled and shook his head.). Within a few hours there were three kayak skeletons on the beach. Lying next to each was a different colored skin: red, orange, and yellow. The passerby from earlier happened back by, gave a smile, and said, "Well, they're the right shape at least." Thanks.

More Problems

The unspoken excitement was building to a pinnacle. The hard part was done, and we simply needed to put the icing on the cake and then head out to sea. In keeping with the script that required any kind of progress to be met by adversity, everything came to a halt when we tried to zip the skins around the frame. As both a positive and a negative, the skins were extremely tight. Had we had more time to test and evaluate the kayaks, we most likely would have changed a few things, specifically the fit of the skin and the zippers that enclosed the poly skin around the frame. The skin was excessively tight. Too tight. We broke two zipper pulls just trying to get skin around the first frame. Thankfully, Eric had the foresight to bring a few extra zipper pulls. They were brought in case of emergency and we had already blasted through two of them, which left only two that remained. The tension mounted. Sweat began cascading down our bodies as visual confirmation of the rising ambient temperature as well as the creeping skepticism that was enveloping the three of us. Eric would tug at the skin, cuss, wipe sweat, walk away, and repeat. John and I looked out of the side of our eyes at each other and watched helplessly. We were hesitant to try anything without being told it was okay, especially at that make or break juncture.

Down the beach a few young men were standing waist deep in the water casting fishing lines into the incoming surf. Their dark skin, due to years of ultraviolet exposure, and the proficiency with which their lines were flying out and reeling in told me they were not tourists. This was their beach. In a matter of minutes one of them caught an eel. He backed out of the water as he reeled it in: slimy and black, aggressively thrashing side to side. Once on the beach I saw him trying to step on it and pull the hook out of its mouth. He looked over and saw me approaching as he said over and over both to himself and narrating for my benefit, "Yuck. I hate eel." Not one to shy away from conversation, I hurried over to get a closer look. I had questions about fishing, and he had questions about the aluminum monstrosities that were tainting his immaculate beach. We chatted for a few minutes, but he obviously had his hands full. I wished him luck and as I walked away, as if the magnitude of what we were doing suddenly hit him, he pointed out to sea and asked, "You taking them out there?" I, somewhat curiously, nodded. To which he replied with a laugh, "You're crazy." My confidence was declining in direct proportion with each cynical local we encountered.

Back at the boats, things were not going well. John was frustrated and Eric was pacing and mumbling under his breath. We needed a break. Eric deduced that leaving the skins in the sun and allowing them to heat up for a while could give us the stretch we needed to get them closed. That was music to my ears. We had been toiling, sweating, and becoming increasingly agitated with the boats and each other. I decided to grab my snorkel gear and go explore the bay. There is something exhilarating about being out in the ocean all alone.

All at once, just below the surface, you become suddenly aware of your limitations as a land dwelling mammal. You are a guest in their world and are subject to the laws of the jungle. …in the sea. With the nervous excitement of a child, I swam out to examine the part of the bay I had not yet seen; the world below. Schools of Blue Tang and Parrotfish played and fed alongside me. They seemed to be bioluminescent, creating their own neon and beautiful light. The hypnotic state they put me in allowed me to forget for a few minutes the frustrations waiting for me back on land. I later found out that Eric, while stewing on the beach, had seen me out snorkeling and had become furious. Apparently, he had wanted to plug my snorkel until I suffocated, bringing me to a slow and panic-filled death. If others around him aren't as stressed or worried about something as he is, he becomes incensed and wishes bad things upon them. I continued to examine the world below without realizing that my life was in danger and that fantasies of my demise were dancing through Eric's head.

The Kayaks Come Together

After sitting in the sun for an hour, the kayak skins became pliable enough to stretch and with a few minor modifications, the zippers came together. Juxtaposed in the sand of Brewer's Bay, Tortola were the three kayaks of differing colors. They were individually majestic, and allied in their shape and purpose. I was filled with a renewed sense of enthusiasm.

Eric went first. We pulled his kayak to the water's edge where he eased himself into the cockpit. With camera in hand John documented the first launch as I grabbed the bow of Eric's boat to draw him into the open arms of the Caribbean. The weight of the boat sitting in the sand resisted my pull. I inched it out, and with each yank the water assumed more of the load; within moments he was weightless in his buoyancy. I let go and entrusted him to the warm and welcoming ocean. All at once I was filled with the same feeling that Wilbur Wright must have felt when he watched his brother Orville take to the sky; the same feeling that Noah must have experienced when he realized the arc actually floated; and the same shock Casablanca Records must have known after signing a band of four talentless New York guys in make-up and discovering that people actually *bought* the records of KISS. Although slightly wobbly, the orange kayak sliced through the incoming surf with elegance and precision. Our brainchild had become a reality! I pumped a single fist into the air, and my chest filled with pride as I shouted "Yes!" to no one in particular.

In 1903 Orville Wright left the earth and returned 120 feet later into the soft sand of Kill Devil Hills, North Carolina. He defied gravity and was airborne for twelve whole seconds. His flight time beat Eric's maiden cruise time by about seven seconds. The orange kayak listed left, Eric leaned right, and the incoming wave lifted the nose and poured Eric over into the shallows. He popped up and punched the water while his boat floated upside down aimlessly. Eric grabbed his kayak and pulled it up onto the shore. All he muttered was, "I don't know, guys" He began walking circles around the kayak, alternating his glances between the boat and the waves. John and I, waiting until Eric could formulate what he wanted to say, stood in silence.

"It's really unstable," he said.

"Let's try it again," I tossed out with cautious optimism.

"I don't know," he repeated.

We regrouped and sent Eric back out into the salty unknown. Again his bottom teetered from side to side while his torso remained centered. With trepidation he dipped his paddle into the water in front of him and gave a half-hearted pull, first right, then left. Within minutes he was a bright orange speck on an aquamarine bay.

Like a kid jumping on his bicycle to race down to the ball yard, I dragged my kayak into the water and, with carefree abandon, hopped in. Immediately, I understood what he meant about the instability. I felt like a bull rider who was doing his best to keep it all in the middle. My abdominal muscles tightened as I rocked my hips to the opposite side of the boat's momentum. The kayak was long and thin and did not offer much side to side stability. Much like riding a motorcycle, I instinctively deduced that a little speed could actually smooth out the ride. I paddled away from shore and quickly found myself beyond the breakers and paddling out to sea with a giant grin on my face.

Soon John was afloat as well and the three of us were paddling over the surface of the Caribbean Sea. Our bodies were tense with the aquatic equivalent of walking a tightrope. Several times one of us could be heard audibly cursing as the kayak rose and fell with an especially large wave or unaccounted-for swell.

For the next hour, red, orange, and yellow kayaks crisscrossed back and forth across Brewer's Bay, Tortola. The beach was once again vacant, and no boats could be seen out beyond the mouth of the bay. We were alone in the universe. For nearly an hour no world existed beyond the fine sandy beaches and palm trees surrounding us. I had been in love with the ocean for many years, but for the first time I began to understand the elemental bond people develop with her. Weather, water, land, and wind: they are all married in their significance to those who would navigate the sea. They coexist in a fine balance that must be both understood and respected. I was not naïve enough to think that I had any greater grasp or control of any of it, but for the first time in my life, I understood the interrelated significance of these elements.

Lunch time crept up on us, and we congregated back on the shore. In unanimous agreement it was decided we needed to grab some food and refuel our tanks. Over peanut butter sandwiches and tuna from the can, I suggested we spend the remainder of the day in Cane Garden Bay. The thirty or forty minute paddle along the coast would be a good pre-game warm up before we headed out to sea. The boys liked the idea and we sat in the shade washing down our lunch with a few slugs of warm water from the plastic jugs.

We didn't take the full allotted 30 minutes for lunch; anticipation got the better of us. John and I paddled out, still acclimating to the art of propelling forward while maintaining balance. Neither John nor I noticed that we had left Eric behind.

Beyond the bay we were officially far enough off the coast to be "out at sea" and yet still close enough that we felt moderately safe. Suddenly realizing we were only two-thirds accounted for, we decided to hover. I think that was the first time since we had touched down on St. Thomas that I began to weigh the gravity of our situation. I was a cork in a bathtub. I was hovering atop unknown depths of water and unknown life. I was staring out at a small island on the horizon. Beyond that was... more unknown. These are the situations that create epic tales of adventure or tragic ten second news blips on CNN, nestled in between who makes the cheesiest pizzas in America and Motor Trend's top three most reliable automotive cup holders. Our plan seemed like a great idea from the moment of inception, but was now REAL. I was exhilarated and scared all at the same time. Whatever is the chemical name that creates "butterflies" in your stomach, was creating pterodactyls in mine.

John broke my meditation with a generalized observation that probably best summed up the situation: "This is freaking awesome," he said in a calm yet enthusiastic tone. I laughed a little bit because he had broken my profound ponderings with such a seemingly simplistic statement. But he was right: it was freaking awesome.

I was soon busy again wrapping my mind around the fact that some aluminum pipes and a thick tarp were keeping me afloat on the ocean when John pointed out that Eric was nowhere to be found and we should return. We turned back towards shore and began to see the bright orange kayak sitting in the sand like a forgotten shipwreck. We paddled closer and it became obvious that Eric was visibly frustrated as he threw his hands up in the air, kicked at the sand, and muttered sounds that sounded similar to Charlie Brown's teacher – if instead of a teacher she were a truck driver on a drunken bender. He was having issues with his seat and maintaining balance, a painful reminder that we finished construction the night before the trip and had never tested the boats.

Staying Put

We regrouped after Eric's verbal assault on the boats, the ocean, and rocks. During his tantrum, he lost a kick fight with a beach boulder which didn't help the situation. We decided to skip the Cane Garden Bay trip. Instead, we thought it best to spend the rest of the day in the safe confines of Brewer's Bay and acclimate to our unstable crafts. We would break camp first thing in the morning and cross over to Jost Van Dyke where we would set up camp and plot our next move. There was not much of a plan beyond that. Our itinerary had already been blown to hell and the trip so far had been a series of plans and punts. We had surrendered to simply taking it one day at a time.

We had not paid for our campsites and thought we should utilize our time on land to take care of the financial part of our accommodations. The three of us slid into our flip flops, threw on t-shirts, and wandered inland a short distance to the "house" that seemed to be an open air combination bar/kitchen/storage facility/livestock shelter. There was no one inside, and it didn't appear that anyone had been in a while.

A woman was passing by and she asked if she could help us. Eric told her we needed to pay for our campground. She said that it would be $21.40 per night, which seemed like a random number for island pricing, but who was I to judge? As we reached for our money she added, "Per tent." $21.40 per tent?! That meant that our three little tents crammed into one small area of sand cost us over sixty dollars per night. We would definitely need to be moving on. In hindsight I'm thinking that she probably did not even work for the campground but happened to be simply passing by when we asked how much it was to camp. Stupid Americans.

The remainder of the day was filled with awkward paddling and an underlying skepticism regarding the direction of the trip. Yes, we had arrived. Yes, the boats were built. But if we could not load our camping gear on them and stay balanced on top of the water, we would be tethered to Brewer's Bay. We stood at the threshold of the adventure we had been working towards for over a year and faced the possibility of going no further, due to our inability to do a better job of managing the game clock. We failed to allow ourselves time to test the boats during the construction stage.

Anger and frustration brewed just below the surface. We weren't mad at anyone or anything in particular, other than our poor time management skills which might mean our kayaks would not do what we needed them to do. Throughout the evening we all exchanged comments like, "It'll be fine!" Though we didn't speak them out loud, a blanket of doubt and speculation hung over us. Our journey could very realistically become three guys on a weeklong camping trip at the beach. Behind the masked confidence, we knew the morning presented us with a fork in the road, and we were all apprehensive about which direction we were about to take.

I drank alone that night. Eric and John turned in early under the pressure of the momentous morning that was looming. I sat in a rickety white plastic chair in the sand. The stars were the only light in my universe. There was a new heaviness to the warm tropical breezes. Sips from the Cruzan rum bottle took the edge off of my anxiety as the gravity of my thoughts gave way to the weight of my eye-lids. I ambled to my tent and surrendered once again to the intoxicating combination of Caribbean rum and the sound of the waves. I was lulled into an amazingly restful sleep.

CHAPTER 6

Crossing the Ocean

The anticipation of breaking camp, loading our things into the kayaks, and heading out to sea proved greater than any thought or desire to take advantage of a perfect vacation morning by sleeping in. The now familiar muffled sounds of tent zippers and footsteps in the sand informed me that I was, again, the third of three to wake. Still, I took a moment to just lie there. I kept my breaths as quiet as possible in order to hear the ocean. As I contemplated the day's aspirations, disobliging thoughts crept in, snaking their way to the forefront of my brain, making their way past the daydreams of a trio of kayaks cutting through the tranquil Caribbean waters. *What if the zippers break again? What if we have too much stuff to fit in the kayaks? Even if we are able to get them loaded and sealed, are they going to be stable enough to negotiate the waves and currents? Are the sharks around here mean? I heard that sharks have to stay in motion or they die. Do you suppose that's true? There hasn't been a good shark movie since Jaws. When was the last time I saw Jaws? Man, that shark was big and strong. I should have worked out more. We should have tested the boats. We should have started building them sooner.*

Even the random thoughts that made their way into my head were quickly pushed aside by apprehension. I could feel the momentum of the negativity snowball gaining speed and crushing everything in its path. Suddenly it did not matter that I was lying in the sand in one of the most beautiful parts of the world. I was being swept away by the impending apex of the trip. Everything we had done before had led us to that morning. The elements were assembled and in place. But... would they work?

Realizing that I was self-sabotaging, I shook myself out of my repugnant mental whirlpool by opening my eyes for the first time. The world was bright, even for that time of the morning. I noticed, by the volume of the waves crashing on the beach, that either my tent had been moved closer to the water as I slept, or the sea was noticeably more angry that morning. I sat myself up and began to feel the dull back ache from a second night sleeping on the earth. I stretched and crawled for the zippered door. With a slow dramatic pull up and over the zippered arch of my tent door, I eased myself out.

I crawled on all fours into the warm and waiting sand. Once again, John and Eric were abuzz packing up their things and scratching their heads trying to figure out how each of us would squeeze ten pounds of shit into our respective five pound bags. Eric had already started a "leave behind" pile of items that weren't going to make the trip. There was a cordless screwdriver, a book, some extra aluminum, and a handful of random items that were axed on the first round of cuts.

As usual, I was not about to attempt as much as a morning yawn without digging through my food bag for some grub. I grabbed a breakfast bar, a multivitamin, a cup of pudding, and a few hits of tepid water from my trusty plastic jug. I sat in one of the white plastic chairs in silence. Neither Eric nor John acknowledged me, nor I them. We moved about each other as if the others did not exist; we were apparitions in a choreographed dance performed by pasty, out of shape men, wandering around stiffly because of a few nights sleeping on the ground. We were submersed in our own mind games. Everyone's train of thought had the same destination, but a different route. While consuming my preservative packed breakfast, I was unconsciously analyzing our environment. I looked beyond the guys and into the bay.

Instinctively, I scrutinized the weather. It is amazing to me, when one's day is so intimately involved with the elements, how the weather becomes a perpetual topic of conversation and a source of constant critical evaluation. *Warm and sunny. Sporadic clouds. Can't see the sky to the east from my vantage point. The water isn't calm, but does not appear to be overwhelming. The wind is mild.* The horizon was inviting. That day, for either the granting of three men's farcical wishes or, for His own personal entertainment, God wanted us to cross the ocean.

I was doing my best to maintain some attempt at personal hygiene. I was already becoming proficient at common tasks in my new simplistic and rudimentary lifestyle. I performed a thorough water bottle tooth brushing exercise as I walked down to the water. Then, probably in vain, I executed a coastal camping bath (I walked out into the water, rubbed my body a little bit, walked out, drip dried, and then applied deodorant).

We all packed, downsized, broke down, wrapped up, folded up, threw away, put away, dry bagged, and squeezed our entire supply of food, water, clothing, shelter, and various supplies into the 18 foot kayaks. In my mind, I had cut my gear down to what I thought was an absolute minimum. I had a few changes of clothing, a few jugs of water, a bag of food, a small backpack sized tent, mask/snorkel, and the canvas bag containing it all. I had a few other odds and ends and a "ditch bag" (that contained the essential things: wallet, passport, iPod, knife, lighter, sun block, and my camera). It was a real life game of survival Tetris. I had a specific sized container and a specific number of various sized pieces that needed to fit in that container. I carefully placed each item into the kayak one dry bag and jug of water at a time until the maximum allowable space was full. I stood up and stepped back to admire with pride my condensed and portable life. There was not a free inch of space and everything fit! Or so I thought until I looked behind me and saw three or four things still lying in the sand, mocking me. I unpacked everything and repacked them in a different arrangement. I still could not make it all fit.

I conceded that I could not get everything inside the kayak and I was going to have to transport some things on the deck - the kayak equivalent of a roof rack luggage carrier. Eric and John proved to be better at packing than I. Their kayak deck rigging mostly contained safety equipment and little else. Mine was loaded with much more including my bright yellow, bulging, clothing bag. Because of the instability of the boats, I was concerned how the top loading would affect my balance. It later proved to be a non-factor. Finally breaking the silence, John called out, almost jokingly, "Any chance we actually make it to Jost Van Dyke in these things?"

"Mine will. I poked holes in your boats with my knife," Eric fired back.

I jumped in, "Bullshit. You couldn't find your knife."

"Hey guys, has anybody seen myyyy...." John mocked, grinning. We all laughed as the mood shifted towards jovial.

Standing knee deep in the water taking in the scenery and pondering the crossing we were about to embark upon, I asked, "Do you think it's a sign that all the locals think we're crazy?"

Eric quickly replied, "I think running out of parts and time, not being able to test the boats, John's flight being canceled, the boats not wanting to come together, the zippers breaking, and struggling to keep the top of the boats on top of the water in calm water are signs. The locals? Naa. They just don't know anything about fine watercraft."

Departure

In the sand of Brewer's Bay, Tortola lay three kayaks, the tops of each adorned a different color: one red, one orange, and one yellow. Each one had been transported from a fire station daydream to their manufacture in a garage in Shawnee, Kansas, and then to the beach in the British Virgin Islands. Now constructed, they decorated the bay, loaded with supplies, and each pointing toward the sea. The thought was absolutely bewildering: *This is actually happening.*

There are some out there who would see this accomplishment as elementary and unremarkable. Others may consider it foolish and careless. I thought of my three sons; and I hoped that, if nothing else, they would think about my adventure and realize that sometimes the difference between possibility and reality is simply how much of yourself you are willing to put into something. The conversation between Eric and I that hatched the idea could have come and gone, like a million others, and we would have both gone on with our lives, unchanged. Instead, John came aboard, and we went to work to make it happen. If nothing else, at that point (as long as we would survive to tell the story), it was a success and I was very proud.

All morning the shore was being hammered by commanding waves. While the boats were being packed, we were all in agreement we would move down the beach to launch them.

There was a spot in the middle of the bay that seemed the most calm and most logical spot from which to set out. But, once we were ready to go, the incoming waves had slowed enough that we felt comfortable shoving off from where we were, timing our launch so as not to keep getting washed back up on the beach.

Eric nominated himself to be the first to go. It's not that he envisioned himself trailblazing a path across the ocean with John and me in tow. He assumed his balance issues might be the biggest liability and that once we got him centered and in motion, that everything else would go smoothly. A million things were going through his mind at once and not one of them an optimistic thought about what was about to happen. He walked around his boat, adjusting the Velcro, scrutinizing the angles and tightly wrapped skin, and paying special attention to either end, where matching orange duct tape wrapped the kayak points as an extra measure to keep the surrounding water on the outside of the boat rather than in it. I noticed that not once did he look out at the water. It was as if the restless and fickle ocean was the constant. The unknown factor was the simple combination of natural elements and physics. Even the unpredictability was manageable to him.

The bane of Eric's morning was the kayak. He knew that even though the trip was a collective idea and effort, the boats were his. He had found the designs, adjusted them, and taken on the responsibility to research and oversee the construction; and now his efforts were all to be tested. And he had doubts. Everything he had done in relation to the kayaks, he would suddenly do differently.

In a final unintentionally dramatic moment, he pulled his kayak to the water's edge and stood with his back turned to the ocean, facing the hills of the island of Tortola like a boxer in his corner before the fight. He took a mental inventory of his supplies and his surroundings and, when he was ready, said, "OK, let's do this."

3, 2, 1... Blast Off

Eric Gifford is a big man. I don't mean that in a negative way. He's just big. At one time the guys at work nicknamed him "pound cake" because he's just so physically... dense. If Dorothy and her family had held on to Eric during that tornado in *The Wizard of Oz*, they never would have crossed over into the Technicolor part of the story with munchkins, ruby red slippers, and flying monkeys. He would have kept them anchored safely in the dreary sepia plains of Kansas. One of the downsides of being a big, strong, manly man is that one does not easily fit into tight spaces; say, for instance, the cockpit of a kayak.

While still nestled firmly in the sand of Brewer's Bay, Eric squeezed, jostled, and cussed himself into his kayak. The boat rocked side to side as he kicked his linebacker legs into position. Once in place, he quickly scooted his ass forward and backwards a few times like a dog on the living room carpet. He successfully lodged himself in and gave me a nod affirming he was ready to go.

I grabbed the front of his kayak and pulled him forward into the water. It was considerably heavier than before under the load of all of his gear, but once the water assumed the weight, he dipped his paddle in and propelled himself forward into Brewer's Bay. Within minutes he was an orange speck on the turquoise water. Our excitement peaked when we saw that he was afloat and moving forward! Eric was paddling over the ocean and heading away from dry land. I helped John in to the water the same way I helped Eric and did not even bother watching him paddle away. I eagerly dragged my kayak into the water, waited for a few small wave sets to roll in so I could time everything just right, and hopped in. There were a few immediate side to side, expletive inducing moments while I gained my balance, but rather quickly I centered myself and paddled out behind Eric and John.

The water beyond the bay was darker, deeper, and busier than we had experienced in the confines of the bay. It was not treacherous, but it certainly required constant attention to maintain balance. Considering our astounding lack of boat building and sea kayaking experience, things were going surprisingly well. The boats were loaded and still afloat, which was both the most elemental yet critical goal, and we were cutting through the water at a respectable pace.

Our plan was to head west along the northern coast of Tortola. Depending on how our energy levels were holding up, we would consider a stop in Cane Garden Bay or, maybe, the legendary driftwood and sheet metal open air bar called *The Bomba Shack* located in Cappoon's Bay, Tortola. We were forced to acknowledge that if our trip were to include a stop at a beach bar, there would be a good chance we would surface several days later broke and hosting colossal Caribbean hangovers. Even with that in mind, we set out to casually parallel the northern coast of Tortola, stop when we wanted, and at some point, make the several mile crossing over to Jost Van Dyke.

Left side, right side, left side, right. We paddled in line, paralleling the coast about a hundred yards offshore. Left side, right side, left side, right side. The rocky coastline to our left was passing astern at a better than expected pace. After about fifteen minutes I stopped, laid my paddle across my lap to catch my breath, and absorbed the moment. There were dark blurred shapes on the sea floor in the crystal water below me. There were clear, blue skies above me, and tropical Caribbean islands on either side of me. It was overwhelmingly surreal. It was a dream realized for me, like something out of one of the adventure stories I read as a kid.

I think I caught my love of adventure from reading, and I know I caught my love for reading from my mother. I remember as a kid seeing my mom sitting at our kitchen table with a book. Every night she would be in the same chair, the one closest to the off-white wall phone with the fifteen feet of coiled and knotted cord hanging below it, reading her books. Sometimes it would be Steven King. Sometimes it would be Erma Bombeck. Most times I had no idea what her book du jour was, but there she was, every night, approachable yet slightly removed. I have learned so much in life from my mom and one of the countless gifts she has bestowed upon me is the love of reading. It probably began with Dr. Seuss. My mom never warned me that Seuss books are a gateway drug. I soon progressed to the Choose Your Own Adventure series where you, the reader, dictated the direction of the story. You would be given two options, each directing you to a different page, and then you would turn to the corresponding page to learn your fate. I was becoming a book junky. It wasn't long until I was strung out on a few of the classics like *Huckleberry Finn* and *Treasure Island*. Fast forward to adulthood and I was still chasing the dragon with *Over the Edge of the World, Into the Wild*, and *Adrift*. I've never had a preference in the fiction vs. non-fiction debate as long as whatever I was reading took me on an adventure. From my couch I have crossed the ocean, climbed mountains, traversed jungles, and gone *On the Road* with Kerouac and, for as long as I can remember, those stories have stoked a fire in me that has fueled my insatiable wanderlust.

I was sitting on eighteen feet of riveted aircraft aluminum I had formed into the shape of a kayak. In that kayak I was on top of the Caribbean Ocean, and it occurred to me I was writing my own adventure story; it was real, and I was, at that moment, in the heart of it. I looked over at John and Eric, and I doubted they were being as romantic as I was about the whole situation. They were paddling with a purpose and that purpose seemed to be to get the damn paddling over with.

Before we knew it we had reached Cane Garden Bay. We pulled up alongside each other. On our orange, yellow, and red steeds we talked for a few minutes and agreed we were "in the groove." Our inexperience led us to believe we could paddle for the rest of the day fueled by energy bars and the postcard scenery. We pointed our kayaks north and began paddling for the small island of Jost Van Dyke.

Crossing the Ocean

I suppose you could argue that the act of paddling from one island to another isn't exactly "crossing the ocean," yet I'm going to call it that based on the technicality that it is, in fact, what it is, and it sounds more grandiose than "paddled to the next island." And that's what we set out to do. As you traverse the landscape of the ocean, you might think the constant and endless rising and falling would be nausea inducing. On the contrary. You quickly realize there is a rhythm to it. You involuntarily navigate your ever changing terrain. Paddle, paddle, paddle... tighten stomach up and over the wave... paddle, paddle, paddle. Repeat.

Jost Van Dyke was within view. Many of the Virgin Islands look similar and it can be difficult to differentiate. Jost Van Dyke bears a scar across the green hills of the south side of the island that gives it away. The brown line that can be seen for miles bisects the landscape. I have been told that it is both a road leading through the hills of the island and, also, simply a rock ledge. We weren't close enough to discern either way. Jost Van Dyke is the smallest of the four main British Virgin Islands and nestles about three miles northwest of our starting point at Brewer's Bay, Tortola. The most popular legend is that the island is named for the Dutch privateer, and occasional pirate, Joost van Dyk (Somehow, over time, the island lost an "o" in the middle and gained an "e" on the end.) who established a settlement in the BVI during the 1600s, although there is no documented evidence which proves that it is, in fact, named for him. Currently it's a tiny speck of paradise where a few hundred people live on about three square miles of volcanic originated tropical hills.

The sun was high in the cloudless sky and without looking at my watch I could not adequately discern if we had been on the ocean for thirty minutes or thirty hours. I had no real concept of time. It was a strange marriage of hard work and leisure. The only real way to judge space between Tortola and Jost Van Dyke was to look behind us as the big British island started to slowly shrink in our wake.

Progress was slow and the space between the three of us grew languidly. Somewhere in the middle, I noticed Eric was further away from me than I was comfortable with and John was beyond him: a yellow dot in the distance that came into view when the water lifted me and disappeared when it lay me back down. About that same time I noticed that, for every one stroke on the left, I would have to paddle four or five on the right just to keep myself pointed at Jost Van Dyke.

The clandestine current of the sea is deceiving. The water quietly moves you in directions you don't realize unless you have an object on land to verify your position: your towel, the lifeguard stand, the blonde in the red bikini, etc. When you are out on the

open water the only landmarks (if any at all) are on the distant
horizon, and they can be frustratingly misleading. There was a
strong current going left to right, and it was a struggle to remain
pointed in the right direction.

What felt like hours passed. Jost Van Dyke wasn't getting
any closer. I liken it to being on the strip in Las Vegas. "Hey, let's
walk to the *Bellagio*. I can see it from here. It won't take that
long." So you start walking towards the *Bellagio*. Days pass. A
beard begins to grow. Family members are nailing fliers with your
picture to telephone poles. You wrap your shirt around your head
as a makeshift turban for protection from the sun. Looking up,
you notice the *Bellagio* only appears slightly closer than when you
started your expedition. It is distance induced deception. In this
story, Jost Van Dyke is the *Bellagio*. It was only in looking back
that I could see how far I had come. There is a metaphor for life
in there somewhere.

Before departing, we made a pact we would stick together
in case anything were to go wrong. Due to the wind, current, and
our differing abilities, we were unable to maintain close proximity.
We were easily spread out over a mile at that point, and I began to
get concerned. John and Eric continued to drop out of sight with
the rise and fall of my boat. If anything were to go wrong with
any of our boats, there was no way of telling each other, let alone
coming to each other's rescue.

The Caribbean Ocean is far more charming from the white
plastic hotel beach chairs from which most people see it than from
the cockpit of a self-built kayak battling a sustained anxiety about
the weather, the water, blisters, the kayak, the guys, sharks,
sunburn, dehydration, and the big ferry boats crisscrossing
between the islands. I don't think the ferry captains would even
notice the aircraft aluminum from a Kansas kayak being twisted

into a knot and sunk to the bottom of the ocean as they motored over it.

Eventually we approached what we would later learn is Sandy Cay. Due to fatigue I think we all were of the same unspoken mindset we would rendezvous there, rest, and continue on together. It was a small, beautiful, and inviting Cay, probably more so due to the fact we had spent the entire day in a quiet state of suspended distress. Paddling in the ocean was like driving in a severe thunderstorm, your entire body is tense without your conscious intention. Sandy Cay was an oasis, seemingly a stone's throw away from Jost Van Dyke, providing a much needed rest stop. Its perimeter was half jagged, angry rocks and half immaculate postcard style beach. Because I was tired, I nearly tried landing on the unwelcoming rocks. I quickly realized that was a bad idea. The jagged rocks would have torn my kayak to shreds along with my flesh. I found the first sandy spot I could and paddled quickly towards the shore.

Sandy Cay

I was the first to arrive. John was a short distance behind me and Eric was a barely visible spec on the ocean. With the assistance of the waves my kayak buried itself on the beach. I hopped out and immediately sank to my knees in the virginal, soft, snow-like sand. I felt like I was learning to walk for the first time. My legs were shaky and unstable. I walked up the beach to regain sensation in my legs, hoping to feel something beneath me that was not in constant motion. Somehow, among the sound of the trade winds blowing past my ears and the waves hitting the sand, I heard a faint and distant, "Finazzo!!!" I turned toward the water and I could see John's kayak about a hundred yards off shore. But something caught my eye in the surf between where I stood and John's boat. It was my kayak! Apparently the ocean wanted it back and had crept up the beach while my back was turned and stolen it. I ran out into the water and started to swim towards it. As I approached the rogue kayak, a wave lifted it with every intention of sending my boat crashing down on my head. It could have been a split second recollection of the "duck dive" technique I learned during a Hawaiian surfing experience or possibly sheer, instinctive panic, but I opted to dive down under the boat and the wave rather than try to stop it with my face. The wave and the kayak passed over me. I popped up on the other side, swam back to it, and then swam us both to shore.

Now, even more exhausted, I waited in the sand for John. He hit dry land and we noticed that Eric was getting close enough that we could relax a little bit. The two of us seized the opportunity to catch our breath, stretch our legs, and stare out at the amazing shades of blue in the surrounding waters. I stood next to my kayak looking out toward the horizon. I saw Tortola to my left, St. John in front of me, St. Thomas a little further to the right, Jost Van Dyke on my far right and thought, "I can't believe we did this. *We actually did it.*" I experienced an overwhelming sense of accomplishment and a sense of reverence, too. I took a deep, slow breath, looked up to where reality had become the inverse and the sky was now reflecting the water, and I mouthed the words to the higher power responsible for creating all of this and for keeping us safe, "Thank you."

And as quickly as it started, my moment of piety ended. Eric was coming ashore, and I needed to bail water out of my boat and take stock of my supplies to see how they had fared on our first major crossing. Other than taking on a small amount of water, I had made it unscathed. John was almost as lucky. He had lost one shoe from his deck rigging, which presented a somewhat humorous (to me) situation. There are no trash cans on an uninhabited cay, so, not wanting to litter, John was forced to continue stowing a single shoe. *Okay, sitting on my couch in Kansas typing on a laptop right now, I realize this is not quite the knee slapper it seemed to be in the Caribbean, but at the time I thought it was damn funny. Fear and exhaustion do funny things to a man.*

Eric brought his boat up next to John's where we all met and exchanged smiles of achievement. Eric and John decided to find a shady spot to lay down in and take a few minutes to actually enjoy the serenity that the islands offer. I, on the other hand, went exploring. Fatigue took a back seat to my sense of curiosity, and I set off to find out what was back in the trees. I meandered in the foliage where there appeared to be a few worn paths where others had ventured before. As I walked, dozens of lizards scurried in every direction with each step I took. I climbed to the summit of the cay where I found a spot on the north side that was exactly what I was hoping to find. It offered a bird's eye view of the islands from a craggy rock ledge where six or seven pelicans took turns diving into the crashing waves below to grab a snack. I sat and watched for a moment and decided to head back down. On the path, I passed Eric, whose sense of adventure had got the best of him as well. I told him how to find my secret spot and headed back down to the boats.

John was arranging some things on his boat, so I decided to continue taking advantage of the down time. I grabbed my snorkel gear and wandered out into the water in search of sea life (and maybe John's shoe). The water was amazingly beautiful, but there wasn't much happening below the surface other than shifting mounds of white sand, so after about a half an hour I swam back to the beach to find out if the boys were ready to continue on to Jost Van Dyke.

On to JVD

We returned to the sun and surf to resume the next part of our journey. It was a short (approximately thirty minutes) paddle over to the eastern coast of Jost Van Dyke. We began to parallel the coast on our way to Great Harbour when we noticed a change to the east. (The weather comes in from the east down there due to cyclical weather patterns.) It was grey. More importantly, the island of Tortola, which had been clearly in view an hour before, was now engulfed in a dark cloud. It was raining on Tortola and raining hard. Our first nautical friction was about to occur.

Eric, being the wiser of the bunch, called out that we should cut in to the nearest bay and wait out the weather. I, who more times than not rely on instinct rather than logic, was adamant that we continue along the coast and not turn in until we had to. John, being the most apathetic of the group, gave a bold and decisive, "whatever!" Eric and I yelled our opinions back and forth to each other with about forty yards of water and several layers of frustration between us. For obvious reasons he wanted to play it safe and pull out of the water. We were in no hurry. No one was expecting us. Given our experience negotiating oceanic weather, it just made sense. I, on the other hand, felt like we were far enough ahead of it to reach Great Harbour before being in harm's way. I also felt we were close enough to the coast that if I were wrong, we could simply turn towards the shore and find a sandy spot to park. He gave in and trusted my idea which, on this occasion, paid off. What I just described as instinct could just as easily be called dumb luck. Eric's opinion is usually and rightfully the default. But in this case, as I had hoped, the weather stayed to our south and we remained dry as we continued west along the coast of Jost Van Dyke.

The weather was not the only issue we would face on that crossing. As we approached Little Harbour, the final potentially safe place before reaching Great Harbour, the wind was picking up, the water became more restless, and the eastern current that was working against us seemed to be getting stronger. In addition to that, fatigue and frustration were setting in.   Eric, in particular, was growing increasingly frustrated and becoming more and more vocal about it. At one point I think heard him audibly cussing the boat, the wind, the water, the pope, peanut allergies, college basketball, long lines, and the color green. I am not sure what the latter topics had to do with anything, but he was obviously angry. The mother F bombs and adjectives that would cause an oil rig worker to be offended flowed freely and openly. My level of irritation had not boiled over yet as his obviously had. I was still enjoying the ride. I attempted to pick up morale and called out, "Just keep paddling, man. We'll get there!" Eric's reply caught me a little off guard and honestly made me laugh a little bit under my breath: "Don't you think I'm fucking trying, Scott?!?" Wow. He used my first NAME! That meant he was really mad, and I was in trouble. Needless to say Eric, John, and I kept paddling. The anger subsided as we breached the mouth of Great Harbour and paddled through the calm crystal waters towards the sandy shore.

We first made land on Great Harbour, Jost Van Dyke in front of *Foxy's Bar*, a Caribbean landmark. A single unassuming jetty stretched out into the harbour that guided us in to shore. Behind it, shrouded in swaying palm trees, was the open air bar and restaurant named for Jost Van Dyke's most recognized bartender, singer, and fun ambassador Foxy Callwood. Because it was still hurricane season, *Foxy's* was not yet open though Foxy himself was wandering through the bar. I approached and introduced myself and the guys to Foxy. He offered a warm smile, some very funny, yet offensive, racial jokes, and presented us each a Bud Light. I have consumed beer in many, many different cities around the world. After drinking nothing but warm water for several days and crossing the ocean in a self-built boat, I can say the best beer in the entire world is the Bud Light at *Foxy's*. He was nice enough to walk us around the bar and even took us around back where the local high school kids were building a sloop (A sloop is a sailboat with a single mast. They have one mainsail aft of the mast and a single head-sail.). Lying in the grass was what Foxy called an "island dog". "You know how I can tell he's an island dog? He's black, he doesn't know who is daddy is, and he sits on his ass all day." Foxy let out a contagious belly laugh at his own joke. He is a famous host and entertainer and for good reason. We three white guys gave an awkward forced chuckle to the black man who was telling racially offensive jokes towards his own race. It's his place and his humor. He was having a good time, so beyond the awkwardness, we were too.

After the tour and the beers, we thanked Foxy and promised to return at a later point; and we wandered down the path of small bars that line the narrow shore of Great Harbour in search of hot food. We found a single place that had just the combination we were looking for: a place that was open and had someone there willing to serve us food. Perfect! The three of us were the obvious tourists. There were a dozen or so people wandering on and around the wood and sheet metal shanties that serve food and drinks during the tourist season. We were fortunate to find one that was open. We each ordered a cheeseburger, fries, and a Coke. Like the Bud Light at *Foxy's*, those may have been the best cheeseburgers we had ever eaten.

After about an hour or two in Great Harbour, our bellies were full and our muscles had returned to normal function. We mustered up the strength to endure one last trip for the day. We needed to get around to the next bay. *Ivan's Stress Free*

Campground located in White Bay was our destination for the day. The paddle there was brief, beautiful, and relatively uneventful.

We made shore together at Ivan's, tied our boats off, and went in search of Ivan. We wanted to set up camp so we could finally and fully relax for the day. After locating Ivan, another Virgin Islands legend, at the bar, we inquired about camping. Ivan's words were soft spoken and mumbled. He moved a lot like Brewer's Bay Carl. What we could discern was that it would be twenty dollars per tent per night. Or we could rent a cabin for sixty five dollars. So, for sixty dollars we could unpack, set up, move in, sleep, tear down, and repack our tents; or we could pay sixty five dollars and sleep in a cabin bed. Being the really, really smart guys that we are, we deduced that for five extra dollars the cabins may be the better option.

"Mister Ivan, we'll take a cabin please!"

The cabin was not quite ready yet. I got the feeling they are never ready until someone wants to occupy them. Then, and only then, will the cleaning staff (most certainly one person who is a relative of Ivan) ready the cabin. While it was being prepared, we followed the path over to the famous *Soggy Dollar Bar*.

There is a gravel trail that leads up and over a hill that connects the two halves of White Bay. From the water, the hill looks like a large arched rock wall. The trail is only evident if you ask a local or happen upon it as you walk the beach. We walked up and over, conversing about the beauty of Jost Van Dyke. We hadn't yet taken time to celebrate our accomplishment or plot our next move. We were on dry land, done paddling for the night, and wanted a drink.

The *Soggy Dollar Bar* is the self-proclaimed birthplace of the popular rum based drink: the *Painkiller*. It is a small little open air bar that is a necessary visit for anyone in the Virgin Islands. Three firemen from Kansas walked in to the *Soggy Dollar Bar* in White Bay, Jost Van Dyke in the British Virgin Islands. I ordered three Painkillers (for the record, that was one for each of us, not all three for myself) and we sat, watched the scenery, and drank. And then drank some more. And then, well, you get the picture. It was there John found true happiness. There is a small hotel there, beautiful scenery, and (most importantly to John) food, drinks, and service. He immediately vowed to return. ...or maybe to never leave.

We raised our small white plastic cups and toasted our achievement. Throughout the trip we celebrated small and large victories. We had traveled to the Virgin Islands, cleared ourselves and our boats through customs, put the boats together, and we had crossed the sea from Tortola to Jost Van Dyke. It was time to celebrate. Although, honestly, we were looking for any justifiable reason to toast. The boats float - let's drink! Everyone had successful bowel movements - let's drink! Hey, there's rum nearby - let's drink!

After three or four rounds of *Painkillers* we decided to ensure our lodging for the night. So we sadly said goodbye to the *Soggy Dollar Bar* and went back to Ivan's where our cabin was ready and inviting, as inviting as a painted plywood shack with two dirty beds can be. The rain had finally found us. As it began to sprinkle, we retrieved valuables and necessities from our boats. Several days into our adventure we realized that everything we owned, whether by sea or by rain, was perpetually wet; and we vented our frustrations about this daily.

Due to the fact that every one of the dozen beach bar/diners in White Bay were closed, we were forced to enjoy another canned meat dinner retrieved from our kayak food bags. We gathered up our food and settled in to the dimly lit *Ivan's Stress Free Bar* where the only other patron was a marijuana smoking grandma who gave us her unsolicited take on island life.

We discussed the next day's course of action over cans of Spam and peanut butter crackers before retiring back to our cabin. Inside the cabin there was one small detail that caught all of our attention simultaneously. A quick game of rock, paper, scissors determined the sleeping arrangements of three guys and two beds. (I will simply offer the advice to "throw what you know" and you will be the one sleeping alone in a bed while the other two guys are in the adjacent bed. ...and it was sweet!)

The cabin turned out to be more of a blessing than we initially realized when, about one o'clock in the morning, I woke to the slow gentle tapping of rain that quickly grew into a relentless driving storm that did not let up for the rest of the night. Though our intentions for the trip were to rough it, we were all okay cheating for that one night. That day we had covered a lot of distance and had accomplished what we came to do. Everything beyond this point was going to be somewhat impulsive and would change with the weather and our moods. We could go wherever and do whatever we wanted

CHAPTER 7

The Adventure Takes a Turn

Under normal circumstances waking to the gentle tapping of rain on the roof is enough to induce a deep, happy sigh and a blissful return to sleep. But when you're on a small island in the Caribbean and your day is dictated by the weather, morning rain can cause stress and trepidation. I lay in bed listening to it. The rain was a light, but steady presence. I knew we wouldn't be going anywhere anytime soon, so I remained motionless on the old, thin mattress trying to ignore the nagging pessimism slithering through my mind.

After the rain, the next sound I heard was a giggle and Eric saying, "Sorry about last night, dude." As if in a movie, everything around me froze and I turned, looked at the camera, and raised a single eyebrow in terrified curiosity. I eased one eye open and cautiously turned my head to face the other bed. I wasn't sure what I would see, and I was pretty sure that whatever it was, I would wish I hadn't.

Eric continued, "I woke up last night and had my arm across you."

John replied, "I must have slept through it because if I had been awake, you would be dead right now." I was glad to have my own bed.

Eric opened the door to a predominantly grey morning. Everything beyond the threshold was dripping with fresh rain water. The calm smell of rain combined with the salty air of the ocean was intoxicating. This refreshing fragrance was enough to overcome the odor of a stale cabin and two musty mattresses, mattresses which had likely played host to unscrupulous activities I shudder to imagine. John and I stepped out onto the covered porch where the clothes that we had set out to dry the night before were now completely saturated with rain water.

"Well, shit," John commented, scrutinizing the dripping shirts and shorts hanging on the makeshift clothes line. He began to chuckle, "If we end up stuck here for the rest of the trip, I wouldn't even be a little bit mad." Over the course of the last twelve hours, the three of us had fallen in love with Jost Van Dyke's beauty and laid back attitude. It possessed pristine beaches, clear water, palm trees, tropical drinks, island music, and its inhabitants shared the happiness of being removed from the real world in a sort of dream-like paradise. If you ever think of disappearing off the grid for a while, Jost Van Dyke may be just the place to do it. While I was beginning to wonder about our next move, I think John was wondering how to get his wife and daughters down to him because he was never going home. He joined me in silence as I stared out at the grey that shrouded the horizon and asked, "Well, what do you think?"

The air among the palm trees was calm and affable, but the rain persisted. We knew two things for sure: we would not be launching the kayaks any time soon and we needed breakfast. Before we left the cabin, I pulled an airplane bottle of Cruzan rum out of my backpack and kept up with my tradition of breakfast rum. Before you assign my newly developed drinking habits as "problematic," allow me to explain.

Several years ago, I had a supervisor at the fire department whom I blame for my morning habit. Captain Julie Harper and her husband Donnie, also a firefighter, have an affinity for tropical destinations as strong as mine. One year, after a trip to the Bahamas, Julie brought me back a Kalik brand beer bottle. The beer had been consumed and she had loaded it with Bahamas' sand. "You couldn't go to the beach, so we brought the beach to you," she explained. What was supposed to be a kind gesture gave birth to an idea. Since then, every time I go to a beach, I bring back a bottle of sand. While in the islands, we were at a new location almost every morning, so I needed a constant supply of small bottles for my sand collection. And because I can rationally justify the need to fill bottles with sand, my rum consumption became strictly pragmatic and functional. That's what I tell my Alcoholics Anonymous sponsor, anyway.

We planned to take full advantage of our location and, in unanimous agreement, we walked to the *Soggy Dollar Bar* for a hot breakfast. I'm not going to lie, the idea of a warm breakfast was more than appealing to me. We walked along the beach to the west and followed the path up and over the rocky hill that separates *Ivan's* from the rest of the bars and diners of White Bay. Part of the path was paved with native, volcanic rock. Other parts were wet and uneven surfaces fashioned by random rocks and sand that made for a challenging stroll in flip flops. Other than my spot of rum, we were stone cold sober and stumbling along like we had just closed the bar down. I have no idea how the local drunks traverse this path. I can only assume they do it often enough that the journey has become instinctive.

Once over the hill, we shuffled into the *Soggy Dollar Bar* and ordered breakfast. I don't mean I had the Key West Omelet,

Eric a short stack, and John a #6 breakfast combo with an extra side of corned beef hash. No, we ordered the single option, "breakfast" from the menu. If you wanted to eat that morning, you were eating "breakfast," and you received what they were cooking.. It turned out to be a good breakfast consisting of a couple of scrambled eggs, a johnny cake (A johnny cake is a cornmeal flatbread - kind of a cross between a biscuit and pancake.) and bacon. "Breakfast" was just enough to fill us up with the first warm morning meal we had eaten on the trip. Sitting next to us was a young couple from Switzerland who were vacationing in the islands with no real itinerary. They said they were staying on Jost Van Dyke until they decided to go somewhere else. They would return home when their money ran out or they were bored. They had been unintentionally following us, or us them. Their tent was near our cabin, we saw them at the *Soggy Dollar Bar* yesterday, *Ivan's* last night, and again at the *Soggy Dollar* today. We learned the Virgin Islands are not just an American escape, but a host to expatriates and sun worshipers from all over the world.

The Weather Intervenes

Because the rain was still an impenetrable hindrance, we set noon as our cutoff time. If we could not depart by 12:00, we would be forced to write off the day and try again tomorrow. Wrapping up breakfast, one by one, we dropped out of conversation and fell into pensively staring at the ocean. In a short time, we saw a change begin to occur. As if the gods were coming around, the clouds gave way and the sun broke through providing the perfect light and temperature for a flawless tropical morning. After paying the bill we walked down to the beach, made small talk, and kept looking out over the sea with a new sense of vision. The water, although beautiful, was no longer scenery. It was terrain that required contemplation, planning, foresight, and respect.

That day was like most days of the trip. Nothing went according to plan. From the beginning, our itinerary changed daily. The initial plan was to begin on the island of Virgin Gorda and then paddle southwest through a long chain of small islands, making our way back towards St. Thomas. Uncontrollable or unforeseen issues forced us to perpetually alter our plans. Our latest goal was to spend the day crossing from Jost Van Dyke over to Great Thatch Island where we would rest and regroup. The remainder of the day was to be spent paddling to St. John where we would spend the night. We then planned to spend the following few days circumnavigating St. John and eventually crossing over to Norman Island (which, according to legend, inspired Robert Louis Stevenson to write *Treasure Island*).

The weather began to change in our favor. We walked back over to *Ivan's* where we packed up our things and loaded up the kayaks. From our previous day's paddle, we had already learned a few things about packing. I learned to keep the food bag within reach, to keep a flashlight and a knife in my "ditch bag," and to keep my bilge pump easily accessible. Bundling up our things we sensed another change in the weather. The wind picked up and grey clouds returned, creeping in from the east.

We each had duct tape that matched the color of our kayaks. Mine was red, Eric's was orange, and John's was yellow. At either end where the kayaks came to a point were potential points of entry for water, so we duct taped them. The matching colors helped camouflage the white trash-ness of using duct tape. We were finishing up the loading process by taping the ends as the one final precaution to keep our stowed cargo dry. That is when the sky opened up and rained out any plans for an early departure. Knowing our plans had, again, changed, we identified what needed to be done: rum. We walked up the beach to *Ivan's* bar.

At this point I should describe what makes *Ivan's* so unique. *Ivan's Stress Free Bar* is an open air bar that is decorated with faded pictures of visiting tourists and celebrities. There are weathered pictures of Kenny Chesney, Jimmy Buffet, and Keith Richards, to name a few. The spaces on the walls between the pictures are covered with glued sea shells and black marker graffiti. The ambiance is, as John would put it, "no worries, mon." The "stress free" part is the bar itself. The small bar has two coolers full of varying kinds of beer behind it, and a couple of shelves on the rear wall filled with liquor bottles. Located on a shelf below the bar is the bottom half of an old Plano tackle box. A small rectangular sign that reads "Cash box" in black marker is taped to it. A price list for general drinks written in ink pen is taped to the wall behind the bar. At *Ivan's* you pay on the honor system. There is no bartender and no waiter or waitress. You serve yourself. The beauty of Ivan's system is that most people who use the bar include a tip, out of habit I suppose, so when they throw money into the cash box, he makes more money than if he had hired someone to tend the bar.

We waited out the weather with some cool, adult beverages while we worked out alternate plans in case we were rained out and completely lost the day. After about an hour, the rain let up and the sky appeared to be more blue than grey. We foolishly had mistaken sunshine for our window of opportunity and hurried down to the beach.

We quickly re-checked our equipment. Although wet, everything was stowed, sealed, lashed, and ready to go. A local man walked by and told us not to head out to sea that day. "It's too dangerous," he said. "I am police. If you go I arrest you." He smiled as he said it, but his warning was meant to be taken seriously. We promised him we would be safe. He shook his head, smiled, and headed towards the bar. If you're reading this at home and thinking, "How many warnings do you need?" you have a point. In hindsight, the apparent answer is fifty-three because I think we had fifty-two warnings and opportunities to realize, just maybe, we were in over our heads, figuratively speaking for the moment.

Great Thatch Island Here We Come

Eric requested to shove off first because he had been the slowest paddler and that would give him the benefit of a head start. With the expertise, but not quite the grace, of an Olympic athlete, he pulled his kayak in to the water, eased in, and paddled away. He quickly cut through the incoming tide and was headed out to sea. John and I were not far behind him. The excitement was exhilarating. We paddled side by side through the water with ferocity. It was like riding a bicycle at that point. If, you know, the bicycle were a kayak. Left, right, left, right...

Between 1492 and 1503 Christopher Columbus sailed four different voyages between Spain and the Americas. His first voyage departed from Palos de la Frontera, Spain and made a brief stop in the Canary Islands where he stopped for provisions en route to the New World. It was about a nine hundred mile journey. After he, with his fleet of ships, landed, restocked and departed the Canary Islands on their way to what would be The Bahamas, I imagine him feeling like he had found his groove and confidently thinking, "I got this." I can't speak for Eric, but John and I were Christopher Columbus leaving the Canary Islands. "We got this."

We noticed Eric's head start was diminishing. A lot. In fact, he appeared to be stopped just beyond the bay. When we caught up to him, it was obvious why he had stopped. From that vantage point, we could see clearly to the east where rain was falling. A *lot* of rain was falling. An attempted crossing at that point would be foolish, so we headed back to the security of White

Bay, Jost Van Dyke. The closer that we paddled to the shore, the harder the rain was falling. By the time we hit the beach we were caught in a tropical downpour.

Back to the Bar

We went back to the bar.

Rain Delay ...Again

The next hour was spent waiting out the weather under the protection, once again, of Ivan's bar. We agreed that once the weather broke (note our optimism), we would wait an additional thirty minutes before attempting another venture out to sea. That should allow sufficient time for the front to pass and the waters to calm. In retrospect, it's funny how our thought processes were based solely on what made sense to our Midwestern brains rather than nautical experience or knowledge. Our noon deadline came and went, but since our kayaks were already loaded we justified pushing back the cutoff and told ourselves we were okay adding some additional time. One o'clock arrived and the sun burned through the clouds with enough vigor that our thirty minute wait lasted about ten minutes. The three of us scurried down to the beach and shoved off again.

Once we had paddled beyond the protected waters of the bay, an immediate and noticeable change occurred. The water was darker and deeper, even menacing. It began to rise and fall in an inconsistent pattern. We could not get in to any kind of rhythm. The kayaks lifted with the swells and, as they began to fall, another one would hit. The waves were erratic. The wind became much more of a factor. Each time my boat would rise and fall with a swell, my core would tighten, my feet would press hard against the foot pegs, and I would loudly make that throaty grunt sound that people make when getting punched in the stomach.

Rather than set my own pace and paddle hard until I reached shore, I opted to do a better job of staying with the group. On the crossing to Jost Van Dyke we had allowed too much distance between us. It wasn't safe. In reality, nothing we were doing was safe, but we wanted to keep the odds as close to being in our favor as we could.

I stayed back a little bit as John and Eric pulled out ahead of me. My goal was to stay behind them, but close enough that we could hear each other scream for help in the event of a sinking kayak or ravenous shark with an appetite for pasty flesh that tastes like bad decisions. It was about an hour later that I started to notice a more favorable change in the weather. The sky became royal blue and the islands in the distance were crisp shades of green due to the foliage that provides their canopy. The kayak had become like a part of me. I was no longer grunting with each swell. In fact, I noticed I was even able to relax a little bit. Hovering somewhere in the middle of the numerous islands I stopped paddling for the first time, took a drink of water, and even snapped a few pictures.

By that time Eric and John were probably a half a mile ahead of me. It was time for me to pick up my paddling cadence a little bit and catch up. I began to see random items floating in their wake. Among other things there was an empty water bottle and our nautical map of the islands. It was flotsam from Eric's kayak. After about thirty or forty minutes of hard paddling, I was close enough to see that Eric was caught in a repetitive series of paddle, pump out water, repeat. He was understandably frustrated. He could not get any kind of consistent momentum because he kept having to bail out water. John noticed I was approaching Eric and decided he would continue on towards Great Thatch, motivated by the desire to forge ahead and find a sandy place for us to pull in as well as an overwhelming drive to be done paddling. There was a "saddle", or a depression in the hill, that makes up the center of the island. That was our new goal. "Go for the saddle!" we called out repeatedly between the three of us.

The closer I was to Eric, the more his frustration became obvious. He was doing a much better job of keeping his frustrations at bay than the day before. I was not the recipient of a single F bomb, derogatory comment regarding my mother, or the intended target of projectiles coming from his kayak. This is progress. His boat was sitting low in the water and with each wave that swept across his deck, more water was pouring in to his cockpit. I saw him slam his paddle down, take a deep breath and drop his head. He pulled out his bilge pump and pumped with the ferocity of a man about to break. He was tired and he was pissed off. I paddled up next to him.

"Something is wrong," he stated.

"What?"

"I don't know, man. I'm taking on a lot of water."

"Maybe you're eating too much salt."

Either I was using humor as a way of defusing tension or I had failed to recognize that Eric was angry, tired, and maybe a little bit scared; but I soon understood when he didn't reply. We have spent enough days and nights together in the fire station and on call scenes to recognize verbal and non-verbal cues. He was stressed.

"I don't know if I can make it, man. I'm taking on too much water. It's not coming in over the top. It has to be one of the seams. I just can't seem to get ahead of it." Because of the design of our kayaks there was no way I could take him aboard nor could I salvage anything and risk weighing down my boat.

The best I would be able to do, if needed, would be to throw him my life jacket and paddle beside him until we both made shore.

Eric kept his composure, relative to the day before, and continued to muscle through an extremely difficult crossing. John had become a bright yellow dot on the horizon that appeared to be at or near the shore. It was difficult to tell from as far out as we still were. As we came closer to the shore, Eric noticed that John appeared to be in trouble. We still could not tell if he was in his boat or on land but the bright yellow kayak appeared to be caught and tossed about on the waves in front of us. Eric had gained control of his boat and was keeping ahead of the constant intake of water. His focus had shifted from anger to concern for John. After assuring me he would be okay, I left him and paddled as hard as I could toward the shore.

Trouble

I approached Great Thatch and noticed it appeared to be an island of rocky shore surrounding a thick wooded mountain. It stretched out in front of me maybe a mile wide. There was not much that was inviting about it. It took me about twenty minutes of hard paddling to get close enough to see that John was standing in the surf and struggling with his kayak as the waves were driving him and his boat onto the rocky shore. Having enough experience with water, I knew not to get too close. When someone is caught by the water in that type of situation it is easy to get drawn in and caught in it as well. It was best to keep a safe distance so as not to become a part of the problem. I brought my boat in close enough that John and I could communicate without yelling, but not so close as to need Eric to rescue the both of us.

All John could say was, "I just couldn't paddle anymore. I needed to get to shore. I think I fucked up." He was standing in waist deep water about ten feet from the shore. Regardless of the many ways he was attempting to enter the cockpit, the pounding waves were relentless and would not allow it. He was under attack and his foe was not letting up. The rocks and coral were cutting up his feet and he was battling fatigue as he attempted over and over to gain control of his boat. It was a losing battle but he was not throwing in the towel. I paddled dangerously close to him. We talked about and tried several different options, but we could not seem to get him back in his kayak. A bad feeling started to sink its claws into me.

Eric paddled up and with about a hundred feet between us, I yelled an explanation of the situation to him. It was about 4:30 in the evening. We only had approximately two hours of daylight left and were in a real predicament. I told him if he would stay with John, I would paddle around the east side of the island and try to scout out a sandy beach where we could safely go ashore. None of us were keen on the idea of separating, but given our available options it seemed like the most logical plan.

Separation

I reluctantly but emergently set out in search of sand. In a tropical paradise like the Virgin Islands, it seems ludicrous to have to go in search of a sandy beach. Make no mistake, there are plenty of pristine sandy beaches; just none where we needed them and, of course, we needed them on this occasion. For about thirty minutes I followed the coast line along the north side of Great Thatch to get around to the east side of the island. The paddle was amazingly pleasant. The water was bumpy but not treacherous. The sun was shining but dropping (too quickly for my comfort) behind me to the west. If my two friends behind me weren't colossally screwed and in need of help, I would have been having a really nice day.

I rounded the corner to the east side of the island and things changed in a hurry. The narrow pass between Great Thatch Island and Tortola caused extremely turbulent water near the coast of Great Thatch. I would like to say my superior physical attributes along with survival instincts allowed me to sustain the perilous journey. The truth is I paddled out of sheer unrelenting fear. I was in, by far, the roughest water I had ever been in. My boat would rise on a wave, start to drop off the back side, and then get hit again by another wave. There was no pattern; it was a constant barrage of angry surf. I was taking on water from all sides. Over and over again waves crashed across the kayak. I thought I was going to lose everything I had stored on my deck. My entire body was tense. I do not recall any thoughts other than to stay in motion.

I have no idea how long it took to pass Great Thatch. However, once I had pulled out of the turbulence and into calmer water, I must have continued to paddle for my life for another ten minutes. By the time I had put the island behind me, I could see Tortola to the east, Little Thatch in front of me, and beyond that was St. John. I thought, "Now I'm really screwed." There was no possible way I could make it back through that mess and there were not enough daylight hours left to attempt circling around the other side of the island. A sinking feeling set in. My friends were stuck on the north side of the island waiting for me to return, and I had no way of getting back to them. I was completely on my own. I didn't have time for much contemplation. I needed to get to shore and set up camp before nightfall.

I saw a beautiful sandy beach straight ahead on Little Thatch. As you would assume, Little Thatch Island is the smaller version of Great Thatch Island and lies southeast of her larger sibling. I paddled hard. I was hoping to make land and dig out my cell phone. I needed to contact Eric and John somehow and tell them not to follow me. Between John's fatigue and Eric's boat issues there was no way they could endure the crossing I had just made. I paddled straight for the beach of Little Thatch. There were a few small buildings there, possibly a main house and a guest house. I began to wonder if anyone was there and if I could find a secluded spot to hide and camp for the night.

My boat slid up on the powdery white sand, and I crawled out. I am sure I presented a scene that, to an observer, must have looked something like a foal trying to stand for the first time or the whiskey drinker at the end of the bar who gets up to go to the bathroom. I was wobbly and awkward. I quickly dug out my phone and, by the grace of God, had a signal. Even though I knew it was in vain, I tried calling Eric first and then John with no luck. I tried calling Eric's wife who could take over calling for me while I figured out just where I was. I had no luck there either. I ended up finally getting ahold of a mutual friend who called Eric's wife for me and relayed the message: "Don't follow Scott. Go west around Great Thatch and meet in Cinnamon Bay tomorrow." It was like throwing a penny into the well, making a wish, and walking away. I had no idea where my message to the cosmos would land.

I put the phone away and sat down in the sand. I felt dizzy with the jumble of thoughts swirling around my head like a tornado. I had about another hour of daylight left. One of my friends was stranded on the rocks of an uninhabited island. The other friend was hovering off shore trying to help him. I had no way of getting to them before dark. I could not communicate with them, and to top it all off, I could see rain over Tortola that was heading towards us all.

My stomach was queasy. Prior to going to the Virgin Islands we understood there was risk. Realistically we had put ourselves in a situation where any one of us could have made a fatal decision or error and paid the ultimate price although I never really felt like our lives were in peril. I just wasn't thinking that way. I knew the risks and considered them to be calculated. Having said that, we had taken those risks and things had gone to hell.

I needed to evaluate the facts of the situation objectively. I was on dry land and safe. They were close enough to Great Thatch Island, they could swim to shore even if it meant abandoning their kayaks. Between the three of us, at least one of us could procure help somehow and ensure the others were rescued. I guess. Hell, I didn't know.

As I was taking stock of the mess we were in and what could be done, I knew one undeniable and agonizing fact: there was no going back for them. I could not make it. There was no time, the weather was turning, and physically I knew I could not go back through the current that had just spit me out. The best thing I could do would be to find a secure place to pitch a tent and then somehow try to contact them to make sure they were okay.

I stood up and went to my kayak to get myself a much needed drink and realized that my water bottle had been swept off the deck at some point. Jesus, really?!? That's just what I needed. I was in trouble. No water. Before I went in search of drinking water, I knew that I had stolen a lot of the ocean and was storing it in my boat. It needed to be removed. I used my bilge pump until every bit of water had been removed.

Out of the corner of my eye I caught something moving to my right. My solitude was suddenly in question. Of all the things I expected to see, I would have to say two little naked blonde haired white kids running towards me along the beach would have to be somewhere near the bottom of the list. But that is what I saw. Following closely behind them was a black woman in her thirties or forties. She smiled and waved, but made no attempt to ask what this stranger was doing on their small island, which made it seem all the more dream-like. I was wearing a backwards ball cap, sunglasses, beard scruff, and swimming shorts. My facial expression had to be a peculiar mix of exhaustion, anger, fear, and curiosity.

I approached her, trying to exude an air of friendliness, and asked if I could camp there. She replied something to the effect that a very rich man was staying there and I would not be allowed to stay. "Much security," she said. I was deflated. I thanked her (doing my best to hide my look of defeat) and walked back towards my kayak. After a few steps I turned back around and asked her if I could get some water from her. She said yes, but I would have to watch the kids while she went to get me a drink.

Let me quickly recap what was happening here: it seemed that this friendly woman was the caretaker of the two little naked kids. Someone had placed their children in her care. With a cordial smile, she had just asked a shirtless, scruffy faced stranger who paddled up onto her island to watch them. I'll just let that sink in for a moment. I agreed to keep an eye on them despite my disbelief I was in the Caribbean on a strange island and my two buddies were stuck out at sea while I was babysitting two strange naked kids.

During my shift as temporary nanny, I dug a t-shirt out of my clothing bag and put it on in a weak attempt to make myself look somewhat presentable. The caretaker returned within a few minutes carrying two large bottles of water and two apples. I must have had a look of disbelief. She smiled as she handed me her gifts. I thanked her profusely and immediately tore into one of the Fuji apples as I prepared to shove off. At this point I resigned myself to the fact I was going to be alone for the night. The sun was setting fast and the rain was still off to the east, but was inching closer. I set off once again with no real idea just where in the hell I was going. I just knew I needed to get there soon.

I paddled around the western point of Little Thatch and headed towards St. John. It was close enough that even from a distance I could analyze the coast. The eastern side of St. John is different than the western side. I was looking at a rocky shore, dense wooded mountains, and not a sign of civilization other than one lone sailboat that was anchored about fifty yards offshore. As St. John grew nearer, my paddle strokes became less aggressive. I was tired. Really tired. My muscles ached, and I still had to deal with the pesky little issues of finding shelter and not knowing if my friends were dead or alive.

I approached the coast of St. John a beaten man. I had been paddling for about four straight hours. Most of those hours were spent paddling in fear of losing my boat, endangering my life, or both. My body hurt, I could feel my pulse in my temples, and I just wanted out of the kayak. The sun was disappearing over St. Thomas to the west, and I still had not found a place I could land my boat. By all accounts it was a gorgeous sunset, the kind that most people on the islands were probably watching while sipping on fruity rum drinks in the comfort of their beach chairs.

I paralleled the coast of St. John for a while. It must have been an hour, but I couldn't say for sure. Time was arbitrary. The only thing that mattered was my deadline: dark. With each point along the coast that I passed, my optimism peaked and, as I rounded each point to find more rocks, my frustration grew exponentially.

The bright blue sky over my head had become a dull grey. Clouds had moved in overhead. The turquoise water had become a dark and menacing foe. I was at an all-time energy low. Several times I stopped paddling, laid my paddle across my lap, and looked around. I was subconsciously praying for something, anything good to happen. Being close to defeat, I could feel my head hanging low. Darkness was beginning to blanket the islands. Tortola, to the east, was a colorless blur because of the falling rain. I looked to the north at what I thought was Great Thatch. (I could not be sure of anything at that point) I saw a small stretch of land that could have been sand, but the low ambient light was playing tricks with my tired eyes. I thought to myself that I would go for it. I would paddle straight for the sand and if the sand proved to be a mirage, I was done. If it were rocks, I would be able to get to land with my life, but my boat would not make it, and I would have to hope for a cell phone signal or a passing boat to save me. Without giving it anymore thought I placed all of my chips on that spot of land and paddled with all that I had left. It was raw desperation.

My strength to paddle came from a spot deep inside of me, a spot that did not want to be stuck out at sea at night during a storm. I call this place my "I don't want to die" spot. It had nothing to do with skill. I was running on sheer adrenaline. I approached the land and, even though it was nearly dark, I could see the small beach was not a mirage. I had never been so happy to see sand.

As I neared the shore, night had crept in over my shoulders, blanketing me in darkness. The rain was beginning to fall, which only intensified the stress though the finish line was in sight. I aligned my kayak to have a straight shot at the beach. I paddled hard trying to gain as much speed as possible in order to plant my boat as far up on the sand as I could. The rain was falling harder as I sliced through the darkness, reaching into my energy reserves, generating momentum. I hit the beach with a coarse slide and was far enough into the sand that the receding water was not able to pull me back. I threw my paddle on the sand ahead of me, hopped out of my boat, and immediately dropped to me knees and threw up. The adrenaline, fear, and hours and hours of paddling had come to a very unromantic ending. I was on my knees, at night, in the rain, all alone on an uninhabited island and vomiting. Not quite the cool climax scene I would like to have played out in the movie of this adventure.

CHAPTER 8

On My Own

I stood up from my little "episode" and immediately scanned the coastline. I spotted an area about thirty yards to the west where sand climbed a bit further up and deeper into the forest, which would allow me to pull my boat, with any luck, out of reach of the tide. I walked out into the water and walked my boat along the coast to the new spot amidst increasing wind and rain. The incoming waves pummeled my weary legs. Slippery rocks under my feet and moving water against my body barely fazed me. I was in a completely altered state of mind. The relocation gave me the benefit of securing my boat to higher ground,

Looking back on my experience that night I can honestly say there is such a thing as survival instinct. I did not consciously plan my next moves. Not for a second did I contemplate what to do next or prioritize my actions for the evening. I just acted. I am saying this not as a credit to me or a self-prescribed ego stroke, but as a testament to our most primal instinct: self-preservation. My boat was too heavy to drag. My remaining strength was limited at best, so I raised the stern and walked a few steps. I raised the bow and walked a few steps, went back to the stern and walked a few steps: see-sawing my way up the beach.

Once I had the kayak up to what I assumed was a safe distance from the water, I pulled my rope bag off the deck and tied the kayak to a nearby sturdy tree. The rain was falling at a steady rate as I grabbed my quick bag (the dry bag clipped in next to the cockpit that held my wallet, passport, iPod, flashlight, knife, a lighter, and sun block). I scampered up into the woods in search of shelter. Fortunately just inside the tree line was a small clearing that was just about the size of my tent. A clear piece of ground in a thick forest was more of a blessing than I could have hoped for at this time. With my flashlight in hand I ran back down in the rain and unzipped my kayak to retrieve my tent. I was shocked. Water filled the lower half of my boat. I have no idea how I stayed afloat. I couldn't figure out if it had come in through the cockpit where I had been sitting, a fault in one of the seams, or a hole in the bottom. I would have to worry about that later. I grabbed my tent, ran up the beach and tossed it in the clearing. I then immediately ran back down for my gifted water bottles and my food bag and ran them up to the clearing. I threw them to the edge of the clearing so I could pitch my tent.

I was keeping dry for the most part thanks to the canopy of trees. It was extremely thick, allowing only light trickles of water to permeate it. If tent building were an Olympic event, I could have come home with a medal. Probably silver. I'm not saying I was the best, but I would have been on the medal podium for sure. I did not even notice the tree branches clawing at my skin as I threaded the poles through the tent and raised it. The tent fit like it was custom made for the small clearing. I tossed in my food and water and then went back down to grab everything off of my deck that might get blown off by the storm, washed off by the waves, or taken by some refugee hiding in the bush who would try to sell my $20 Wal-Mart life jacket on the Virgin Island Craigslist.

Once inside the tent, I sorted all of my easily accessible valuables. Anything that was below deck I was willing to risk because, in all honesty, beyond the basics, I did not care anymore. My clothes were (again) completely saturated. I peeled down to nothing and hung my drenched shorts and shirt on tree branches outside the tent to dry overnight. The world outside my tent was dark. Really dark. Scary dark. Without knowing what might lie in the obscurity around my tent, I opened my knife and kept it right next to me.

It was time to try to get in touch with Eric and John again. By the grace of God, I had a cell phone signal. I rarely had signal anywhere in the islands but I was close enough to St. John to somehow be under their cellular tower umbrella. I called John. No answer. I called Eric. No answer. I called John again. Eric again. I had no luck getting a hold of either of the guys but was able to make contact with Erin, Eric's wife, who said they had been rescued and that was all she really knew at the time. Sigh. Thank God! I didn't know any details, but knowing that we were all okay afforded me the first opportunity of almost the entire day to take a moment and relax.

Taking advantage of my cellular opportunity, I made a few phone calls to let family and loved ones know that I was alive. The funny thing was that no one seemed really surprised we had paddled ourselves into a predicament, and no one seemed surprised that we had managed to come out of it okay. They could not fully comprehend what I had just gone through, and I didn't have the energy to do the story justice. It was time to recover.

Once I was sure Eric and John were okay and I had called those closest to me, my stomach relaxed enough that I knew I should attempt to eat. Other than the apple on Little Thatch, that was the first time I was taking time to eat since breakfast at the *Soggy Dollar Bar* which, at that point, seemed like days ago. Sorting through my bag I picked out a can of something. The label had been washed off so it was anyone's guess what the contents were, but it truly didn't matter. It did not take long to remember my can opener was somewhere under water inside of my kayak. Fortunately, I had one can with a pull top, which made my dinner choice easy.

I tore into what turned out to be spaghetti like a lion that had just tracked down a meal on the Savannah. I washed it down with warm bottled water and thought I might treat myself to a dessert of water saturated M&M's. They were colorless and dripping wet, but tasted like... well... they tasted like shit. I recklessly ate them anyway and was happy to do so.

After about an hour on the island, the rain had stopped and I had food in my belly. Everything had settled down, and I was just happy the critical things had all been taken care of: Shelter – check, food – check, water – check, the other guys were safe – check. I was cautiously content.

My mind began to wander. I wonder what the island looks like in the daytime? What exactly did "Eric and John were rescued" mean, and where were they? What kind of strange animals or people live on small uninhabited islands? More importantly, do any of them eat people? Restlessness was creeping in again as I wondered about my friends and became unsure of my surroundings.

Suddenly, almost on cue, my phone rang. To say that it scared me would be a gross understatement. I almost drove the open knife, which was in my hand at that moment, right through the center of the phone. Looking down, I saw John's name on the caller ID.

I excitedly answered the phone wanting to know what in the world had happened to them.

"Hey man, are you okay?" I asked, rather than leading with the more traditional, "hello".

John laughed, "Hell yes, we're okay. We're on a yacht."

I experienced another movie moment in which everything stops and I look at the camera to have a conversation with audience. I pulled the phone from my head, looked at the fictional camera and mouthed the words "a yacht??"

Still laughing, John explained, "We were rescued by Dutch airline pilots. They keep throwing Heineken at us. They're cooking tuna steaks for us right now. This is the best rescue ever!"

"Is Eric with you?"

"Yeah," he said laughing at something very jovial on his end that I did not understand in my current state of mind. I was having trouble absorbing the facts John had just slurred to me. *John and Eric were rescued by a yacht full of Dutch airline pilots and were currently on said yacht drinking an endless supply of imported beer.*

With all the enthusiasm of a college kid who wants to pick up his frat buddy to come to the party, John continued, "Where in the hell are you? We'll come get you!"

"Man I wouldn't even begin to know where to tell you to look. I'm on some island in my tent." John gave a dismissive laugh. He wasn't going to be bothered with my story. They were safe, I was safe; that was good enough.

"We're playing some drinking game with cups that they taught us. I'll have to show you." I assumed that, apparently, they were so concerned about my well-being, they had had no other alternative than to drown their worry with Dutch pilot drinking games.

John continued, "I think they're going to take us to Tortola. YEAH! I'll take one! Sorry, I need another beer. What are *you* going to do?"

I deduced there was going to be no significant logistical planning happening that night.

So I replied, "I'll call you in the morning and we'll figure it out." He agreed and we hung up.

I tossed my phone into the corner of the tent, laid back and drew a deep breath. My friends were okay. I was okay. But just a moment later, laying back in my quiet tent and looking up into the darkness, the gravity of my situation sank in. If I was correct, I was on the south side of Great Thatch Island. I was alone on an uninhabited island. That was the dream, right? I was alone on an uninhabited island! I didn't even have a single one of the top three records you always talk about with your friends that you should have in that exact situation.

A friend of mine turned me on to the Chuck Klosterman book *Fargo Rock City* in which he claims that on a deserted island he would take the gold re-mastered 24k gold Pink Floyd discs. Klosterman states, "The content of the disc is irrelevant; I simply assume gold would be malleable enough to pound into an arrowhead so I could kill myself a wild boar. Gold is also nice and shiny, which is ideal for bartering with the natives (maybe they could trade me a kayak or something)."

I became restless. I unzipped my tent and stepped out. If you want to know what it looks like on an uninhabited island at night close your eyes, put on a blindfold, and then hold your hands over it. It is dark. I flipped on my flashlight and walked down to the beach. The waves were hitting the shore with a constant rhythm. In true tropical fashion, the storm had blown in and blown out in about an hour. I looked up and the sky looked exactly like I hoped it would. There were more stars than darkness. I could see the lights of St. Thomas to the west. I stood there completely naked on the beach of an uninhabited Caribbean island in silence and awe. That lasted about a minute. Then it dawned on me that I did not know where I was or what else might be there with me. So my moment of awe and wonder was quickly gone, and I hustled back up to the security of my tent. That paper thin tent offered as much security as your bed sheets do from monsters. Those sheets and my paper thin tent were impenetrable to bad guys.

I took a swig of Cruzan from the bottle I had first opened at Brewer's Bay with Eric and John to toast our accomplishments up to that point. I wondered for a moment if that was ironic, but then I lost interest and attempted to write a little bit in my water logged notebook.

The following is the best I can make out from a wet journal written by a shaky hand, cramped and tired:

10/21

22:00 – I am here alone on Great Thatch Island. John and Eric have been rescued by Dutch airline pilots (long story). I am living the deserted island fantasy although it's not much of a fantasy. It's hot. It's lonely. It's creepy. Every noise outside the tent is a footstep. Every gust of wind a whisper. I lay here tired, yet cannot sleep. My entire body throbs with the dull ache of paddling over eleven miles, almost none of which was enjoyable. It felt more like survival half of the time. I find myself taking a moment of pause and reflecting on life and decisions and can't help but wonder how or if this trip will affect me from now on.

Too much to think about right now. My brain, like my body, is exhausted. Time to say a prayer and thank God for our safety today. Tomorrow – Lord willing – Cinnamon Bay.

Fatigue combined with the steady pulse of crashing waves and the sounds of the night forest created a soothing island lullaby. It also created the perfect soundtrack for a horror story. Even for a rational adult, it was a little bit scary. I've since been asked, "Scary? Have you never been camping before?" Yes, I have been camping before. I first went camping with my family when I was three months old and have continued to do so throughout my life. If you don't understand the difference between a camping holiday and my experience alone that night on an unknown island, I encourage you to travel to a foreign country, locate an apparently deserted and unfamiliar island off the coast, travel there alone in the dark, and spend the night. I had no idea who or what else was on that island. I simply knew that I was alone and in a tent with nothing to defend myself but a folding pocket knife. I took a few more sips from my Cruzan rum bottle and pulled my iPod out of the dry bag. Butch Walker's *Letters* album diverted my racing mind and relaxed me. *Closing Time* by Tom Waits finished me off. I fell asleep still sweating, naked, with a headlamp across my forehead, and an open knife in my hand. Try to get that mental picture out of your head.

You're welcome.

CHAPTER 9

An Unlikely Rescue

I have told you my story after I separated myself from the other guys and ended up alone on an uninhabited island. But John and Eric had their own adventures after I left them. It took several years and bribing them with beer to finally persuade them to sit down and give me every detail of their story. What follows is their account:

Crossing from Jost Van Dyke to Great Thatch, John and Eric paddled relatively close to each other while I hovered behind. They were close enough to stay in contact even though they didn't have much to say. John gritted his teeth as he struggled against the current and Eric was busy trying to keep up while bailing water out of his kayak. In fact, he was bailing water at an alarming rate. The water outside of Eric's boat was agreeable, but the water inside of his boat was threatening to capsize him.

The waves were not coming up and over the deck so he knew the water had made it in another way. There was a problem with the boat, most likely a failure of one of the seams. Common sense dictates that this was probably due to the fact that his seams were glued together hours before the departure flight, had never been tested, and were still drying somewhere in the air over the continental United States. Just minor details, really.

Fatigue was beginning to take hold of both of them, and John recognized Eric was struggling with his kayak. Knowing I was approaching from behind, John left Eric and headed towards land to try and find a safe place for us to go ashore. The closer he came to shore, the more he desired to get onto dry land.

With proximity came the ability to recognize features on the island, and John recognized that there wasn't a damn bit of sand on which to land. The island was a giant boulder covered with trees. He immediately became angry at every post card and tropical fantasy that pictured secluded islands. There should have been white sand. There should have been gently swaying palm trees with a vacant hammock swinging between. There should have been an unexplainable fruity rum drink with an umbrella resting on the rim and ice that defies physics by not melting in the tropical sun. Great Thatch Island had none of this. It was bespeckled with ancient volcanic rubble, smooth and rounded by the sea.

John's pot was about to boil over. He was tired from paddling for hours against a formidable current. The respite that the island offered would not come easy. The water near land was turbulent. Waves rocked the boat from side to side and front to back. John was ready to get out and get out soon. He paddled straight for shore thinking the rounded rocks might offer a friendly enough opportunity for him to carefully drag his boat ashore.

In an act of combined bravery and optimism, John jumped out into waist deep water, thinking he would walk his boat the rest of the way to dry land. He looked back out at sea and saw that the red dot and orange dot were together which meant I was there to help Eric, so he could focus on the matter at hand. He was immediately pounded by the constant barrage of incoming waves. They were more powerful than they appeared, and he struggled to keep his balance on the uneven terrain below his bare feet.

The pull of the current drew John to the west where the rocks were not as rounded or smooth. They were less benevolent, sharper, and more jagged. Waves tossed him across the unforgiving sea floor that tore at his flesh. His boat rolled back and forth in the choppy sea as water forced its way into the cockpit. The increasing water weight added to the weight of an eighteen foot boat made maneuvering the kayak almost impossible. John was getting beaten up. The rocks and coral were shredding his feet, and the ocean was using an eighteen foot yellow kayak, filled with supplies and water, to kick his ass.

He recognized he was becoming the victim and decided to take charge. He determined it would be better to climb back in and paddle away from the danger area to more calm water where he could catch his breath and begin troubleshooting. However, every attempt to board his boat resulted in him being rolled right back out. In utter surrender, John resolved to swim the kayak back out to sea where the water wasn't as angry and hold on to it until Eric and I arrived and could help get him to a better place.

Already fatigued, he battled with all of his energy against the incoming waves. He reached up into his boat and grabbed the bilge pump. To keep the kayak away from the shore John kicked his legs and worked the little plastic pump trying to get as much water out of his boat as he could before Eric and I arrived. It was completely futile. For every gallon of water he evacuated, two seemed to take its place. John had rocketed past angry and had become wholly furious. After about thirty minutes of swimming and pumping and pumping and swimming, John saw my red kayak quickly approaching from the north.

Eric

Meanwhile, once Eric had removed most of the water from his leaky vessel, he had been able to rest a while. He was finally sitting in a mostly dry kayak and he need not worry about John because I had paddled ahead to check on him. The water was calm, and Eric could actually enjoy himself again. He paddled with ease, intentionally relishing the moment and taking in the scenery. One thing, though, kept concerning him. From his vantage point, things did not seem to be improving for John, even though he could see I was with him. As quickly as the blissful delight of his current situation had come, it left him. He recognized trouble ahead and picked up the pace.

He paddled up and assessed the situation. After a brief consultation, I paddled away to the east in search of a safe harbour while Eric stayed to help John. Eric sat in his kayak and held John's against it while John continued to bail out water. After forty five minutes attempting to bail water out of a rolling kayak, John slammed his bilge pump into the cockpit in frustration. What they were doing wasn't working, and he needed to figure out what in the hell was going on. He swam up near the bow feeling the underside of the boat just to check the integrity of the skin. Before he made it around the front of his boat, his hand felt something and he knew immediately what it was.

In his mind, what John had felt on the underneath of his boat meant the end of the adventure. Somehow, somewhere he had ripped a hole into his kayak. It was a hole big enough to fit his entire hand. The rocks and coral on the merciless sea floor had taken a piece out of John's kayak and effectively closed the book on any semblance of our original plans that remained.

John did not panic. He didn't cuss, yell, or punch the water. He wasn't even mad. Surprisingly, John felt overwhelming relief. He could then take his boat to shore without fear of consequence. The rocks suddenly didn't matter. At that point what he wanted more than anything was to rest. He had been in an intense struggle for hours, and his body needed to stop and take a break.

Eric subconsciously shared John's relief. He wasn't happy about what John had discovered, but at least there was an explanation. There was a reason they couldn't get the water out of his kayak. He noticed the sun had peaked and was on its downward arc towards nightfall. Also realizing that he too had a boat issue, it occurred to Eric that the adventure was rapidly coming undone. They needed dry land to inspect boats and reevaluate everything.

A plan was devised. John should go ashore and begin salvage operations while Eric headed out in search of sand. John was close enough and had some measure of protection. He felt comfortable on his own allowing Eric to head in search of me and sand.

John

As Eric paddled off in the same direction I had gone an hour before, John pulled his boat up on to dry land. The friction and the abrasive sound of the kayak dragging across the rocks, prior to that day's events, would have induced an immediate halt of operations. But since the damage had already been done, John dragged the boat without regard for anything other than getting the goddamn thing out of the ocean. He fought for every inch of progress. With the added water weight it had become a giant yellow anchor and having two-thirds of it up on land was going to have to be good enough.

John experienced new found energy in his surrender. Without stopping for a break, he immediately went to work breaking down the boat and unpacking. The zippers that had caused us so much stress a few days before were opened up and the skin peeled back, allowing the water to return to the sea.

Imagine the sudden failure of an above ground pool. That is what happened when John peeled the yellow and black skin off of his kayak frame.

He began by separating things. The essential things like his wallet, clothing, and passport along with souvenirs he had picked up on Jost Van Dyke were placed into three "go with me" dry bags. All other nonessential things were placed in the "fuck it/I don't care anymore" bags. In John's mind, Eric and I were together and fine. He was on his own and needed to formulate a plan to get back to civilization where he could then figure out how to locate Eric and me.

It occurred to him that when he had bought souvenirs at the *Soggy Dollar Bar*, he had thrown a business card into his bag. John rifled through his bag 'o souvies and located the card. Somehow he had cell service through almost the entire trip and maintained it on the island that evening, so he decided to call the *Soggy Dollar Bar* in search of someone to come and get him.

"Soggy Dollar Bar."

"Hi. My name is John. I was there this morning and am now over on Great Thatch Island in a kayak. I tore a hole in my boat and am stuck. I was wondering if there is anyone there who would be willing to bring their dinghy over to get me. I'll pay them a hundred bucks - cash."

"Uhhhh...."

John got the sense that the woman taking his call didn't believe him. So he added,

"I'm one of the guys who was there this morning with the three colored kayaks." He reiterated, "I put a hole in my boat. I'm over on Great Thatch, and I need you to find someone to come and get me and take me back over to Jost."

She agreed to ask around, and within minutes John's phone rang. The woman from *The Soggy Dollar Bar* said she had located a guy and that he was on his way. John's elation was quickly squashed when he realized it was pitch black at that point. Night had crept in and an incoming rain storm drew a dark blanket over the Virgin Islands so not even the stars were out to help him see or be seen.

John is an easy going and amazingly sensible guy. He quickly assessed the situation and recognized he was on dry land with a fully charged cell phone and a strong signal. He had a tent, food, and water. He figured that, worst case scenario, he would be camping on a tropical island. No worries, mon.

John resigned himself to the fact that the adventure was over for him. He felt embarrassed, thought he had ruined the trip, and assumed Eric and I would continue on without him. His embarrassment quickly gave way to the fact that he would most likely be spending the remainder of his time in the islands with the comfort of a hotel room, which didn't make him even a little bit upset.

John sat down on a rock and waited for the boat. While he was waiting, he decided to call his wife. He left her a cryptic message saying, "Everything is fine. I'm fine. I have five bars on my phone and food and water. I don't know what you may hear from the other guys or other people, but don't worry; I'm okay and I'll be rescued soon." I can only imagine what was going through her mind after hearing that message.

Several hours passed from the time John pulled his kayak ashore to the moment when he sat alone in the darkness waiting for a rum-drunk yacht owner to steer his inflatable boat over to collect him and the hundred dollar reward. From somewhere out at sea John heard an outboard motor. He shined his flashlight out into the darkness hoping to signal his rescuers and give away his location. The bartender from the *Soggy Dollar Bar* called to see if John had made contact with the dinghy yet. "I can hear a motor and I'm trying to signal, but I can't see anyone yet." Rescue was on its way.

Eric

It was late afternoon when Eric left John to fend for himself. He pointed his kayak to the east and followed the shoreline of Great Thatch. The sun was at his back, and there was just enough of a breeze to keep him cool but not cold. For all intents and purposes it was a perfect afternoon to be kayaking; except for the fact that, you know, one friend disappeared an hour ago and hasn't been heard from since, and the other friend was being left behind to his own devices. Otherwise, the weather and scenery created the perfect setting for kayaking that Eric had envisioned when we first started planning the trip the year before.

As he approached the eastern point of the island that I had traversed earlier, he began to establish a game plan. He would first see if he could locate me. If not, he would find a boat and beg for use of the captain's dinghy (insert your own joke here). He hit the "OK" button on the GPS tracking device because, even though we were separated, the assumption was we were all OK.

However, as he rounded the point of the island and turned south, the water changed. It seemed to come at him from every direction. Eric not only had the stress of staying afloat in the turbulence, but he also had a faulty seam to worry about. He was frantically looking for a safe spot to put in, but he was faced with nothing but sheer rocks and crashing waves. His only thoughts were that if he were to lose the boat, he would be pummeled against the rocks. He had to get away from Great Thatch so he turned sharply to the east and paddled towards Tortola.

The turbulence subsided as he distanced himself from Great Thatch Island, but the cross current was dangerously strong. Although he felt more comfortable out in the open water, it was a struggle to maintain a consistent heading in any direction. Eric knew he needed to get somewhere and do something, but wasn't sure exactly where or what. Great Thatch was behind him. Little Thatch was to his right, which, unbeknownst to him, is where I most likely would have been at that time. Tortola lie directly ahead of him to the east. He only learned this in hindsight. At the time, he was slightly confused and only knew there were islands in nearly every direction and, with a lack of road signs in the middle of the ocean, he set his sights for what would turn out to be Tortola.

A sailboat making the passage into the harbour at West End, Tortola caught his eye and made his decision easy. Where there are boats, there is help. West End is also the home to a ferry boat terminal where large ferry boats haul locals and tourists alike by the dozens back and forth from island to island. As Eric was struggling against the current, he noticed one of the ferry boats heading in his general direction. He turned his kayak towards Little Thatch Island and paddled as hard as he could to get out of the way of the incoming ferry boat. I can only assume that, even factoring in the beauty of the islands, operating an inter-island ferry would become monotonous. One's only joy might conceivably come in the form of scaring the life out of nearly panicked tourists who have built their own kayaks and are paddling in search of help to rescue their lost friends. The ferry cut its angle and passed just behind him in his wake, causing Eric's kayak to rock violently and waves to wash up over his deck, nearly swamping the little orange boat that could.

The previous frustrating routine of paddle, paddle, paddle, bail water, bail water, bail water was once again necessary. He had taken on water from the waves near Great Thatch, the friendly ferry boat, and the leaky seam. Determination was the only thing that kept Eric in motion.

He closed in on Tortola and could see houses up in the hills along the coast and several businesses and docks but no sand. He had found yet another beautiful island in the tropics with no beach. Eric made his way to the back of the harbour and found several boats tied off to moorings, but he decided to approach one of the docks and found the *Bagheera*. He carefully chose her because his discerning eye noticed she was the closest boat that had signs of life.

Eric recognized her flag but didn't spend much time trying to recall whose colors she was flying. He paddled up to the catamaran yacht where three men were lounging in the cockpit and installing a rail mounted barbecue grill. He asked if they knew of anywhere he could rent a dinghy, explaining that he had a friend stranded on Great Thatch who was in need of rescue. Apparently, I had fallen completely off Eric's radar by that point because I didn't get a thought or mention until much later.

He was happy to find the men spoke English. They seemed to be extremely friendly and agreed to rent him a dinghy so he could go fetch John. One of the guys directed him to the dock and hopped out of the boat to help Eric onto it. Eric rolled out of his kayak into the water and was going to swim his boat up to the guy, but he found his legs had fallen asleep at some point during the day and failed to inform his brain, so he was left doing a desperate, modified doggy paddle I would have paid money to see.

The guys were kind enough to grab the kayak for Eric and help up him up on to the dock in what I can only assume was an act of charity for the kayaker who appeared as if he had suffered some kind of spinal injury while out at sea. As one of the men tied off his kayak, Eric struggled to regain sensation in his lower extremities.

The men introduced themselves in English through an unmistakable foreign accent. Eric spent the next five or ten minutes shaking his legs to jump start the nerve endings while he told them our story: what had happened and what he needed. As the conversation continued, a woman appeared from the cockpit of the boat. Natalia had heard what was going on and instructed the men to lower the dinghy and take Eric to pick up John. Natalia was clearly the captain of the boat, and the men did not hesitate to follow her instructions. A few of them began helping Eric onto the Catamaran while one of the men brought the kayak to the rear of the yacht and tied it to the back of the large vessel.

Darkness was settling upon them, so they wasted no time preparing the inflatable dinghy. Partly because they were men with priorities and partly because, despite Eric's situation, they were all still on vacation in the islands, the first of the supplies that was loaded into the dinghy was a more than adequate amount of canned Heineken beer. Natalia handed them a portable VHF radio, already turned on and tuned to the appropriate frequency. They double checked the flashlight to ensure the batteries were good, fired up the outboard motor, and headed out towards Great Thatch.

Rain had begun to fall. The drops felt like BBs peppering their faces; but Eric was so happy he had secured a means to get John, he barely noticed. Again, note that I was not only NOT a priority in this rescue mission, I wasn't even an afterthought.

They approached the island and Eric could just make out the silhouette of the coastline and locate the "notch" in the rocks where he remembered leaving John a few hours before. They hovered about a hundred yards off shore, knowing the rocks near the island were just below the surface of the water and unforgiving. As the boat inched forward, Eric leaned out the front of it with a pole and poked the ground beneath the water to ensure they stayed off the perilous rocks.

They could see no signs of John, or anything else for that matter. They decided to cut the motor, thinking maybe then they would hear him if he were calling out to them. From somewhere in the distance they heard a faint, "Heeeyyyy!!!" Eric called back, "We have a boat. If you can see us, swim out to us." They flipped on the flashlight and scanned the coastline. Fortunately, in no time, John came into view.

In the darkness John had heard the sound of an outboard motor. He had heard it earlier, but it had gone away before he could locate it or be located by it. It sounded close though. As luck would have it, the motor cut out.

"Heeeyyyy!!!" John yelled out.

A light swept across the coast line from the ocean and landed on him. He had been spotted! John grabbed the first of his three dry bags and swam through the warm water towards the light. He approached what he thought was a dinghy brought over from a generous boat captain on Jost Van Dyke. He swam up to the grey boat, tossed his bag inside and was shocked to see Eric leaning over the gunwale smiling and holding a can of beer. In the back of the boat was a Dutch airline pilot named Renz who smiled and raised his Heineken as the international symbol of, "Hey,man. What's up?".

John didn't take much time to try to figure out what had happened or to celebrate their reunion. "In the bag is my phone. Get it out and call the last number on there. It's the *Soggy Dollar Bar*. Tell the bartender to cancel my order. I don't need her to send someone after me." Eric nodded and reached in to the bag for the phone. John swam back to shore to retrieve his other two bags.

Eric reached into the dry bag and grabbed the cell phone. He found the "last number," which was a missed call and hit the call button. It rang a few times but was not picked up by the bartender at the *Soggy Dollar Bar*. On the other end was a lieutenant with the Coast Guard asking if there was an "incident" which required assistance. He asked Eric to identify himself, who was involved, where they were, and what had happened. Eric quickly declined the Coast Guard response saying, "No, everything is fine here. We're accounted for and okay." Once again, note that at that point Eric and John had no idea where I was or whether I was dead or alive. It was night time at sea, a storm had passed by, and they hadn't heard from me in hours. The Coast Guard, who were most likely notified by the *Soggy Dollar Bar* folks, asked if we needed any assistance, and Eric replied, *"No, everything is fine here. We're accounted for and okay."* He was partially correct. THEY were fine and THEY were accounted for. No wonder it took years of bribery to extract the details of their story from them.

Eric and John Together Again

John climbed in the boat with his other two dry bags and Eric immediately tossed him a beer. Their spirits were good. They were going to be okay. They were chauffeured back in to West End by Renz and talked of finding a hotel on Tortola and how they would meet back up with me. THERE I AM! I finally crossed their minds. Still, they seemed unconcerned about my well-being, but rather how they were going to meet back up with me, wherever I had ended up. I suppose it's a compliment they assumed I wouldn't get myself killed, but just a little concern would have been nice.

Before reaching West End, they noticed a light on the water that turned out to be the *Bagheera*. Natalia had given up her primo mooring next to the dock out of concern for her crew mate, her dinghy, and the American who was limping around on the dock due to a possible spinal injury, and she had relocated the yacht from the harbour out to the main channel. The men motored up to the boat and, at the stern of the catamaran, Eric saw his kayak hanging from the dinghy launch. The entire weight of eighteen feet of kayak was hanging from the D rings that we had glued to it hours before departing Kansas. It was bowed heavily in the middle from the weight of Eric's gear and water. He cringed but decided not to mention anything out of fear of seeming ungrateful.

Five or six people were out on the yacht, and they welcomed the dinghy by tossing more beer out to them. Natalia was concerned for both Eric and John and wanted to make sure they were okay. They wrapped John in a towel and made sure that his hands were never without a Heineken. The mood was light and bordered on celebratory. Eric and John, along with Natalia, Renz, and the rest of the Dutch airline crew, threw back beers and laughed and told stories. It was then they informed John that Renz, the guy they had sent out to rescue him, had been drinking all day long and had passed being drunk hours before.

They turned the catamaran back to West End where they found another mooring, tied off, and continued the party. Somewhere in the haze of malted barley and hops, John decided to check on his old buddy Scott. He called and made sure I was okay and informed me that they had planned to head into town with the

Dutch gang, grab some dinner, and find a hotel to crash in. However, he said they had already drunk through that plan and were currently playing drinking games and cooking tuna steaks on the yacht. Actually, I learned all this after the fact; at the time, I barely translated the jist through slurred words and giggles.

Over the course of the evening, two other boats made their way over and tied off to either side of the *Bagheera*. It had officially become a party. Everyone involved was completely drunk. Remember earlier in the story when I mentioned how handy Eric can be? He's the guy that knows something about everything. Eric got word the air conditioner on one of the boats was not working. With all the confidence that beer provides, Eric declared he would be *happy* to fix it.

Eric's "fix" involved a screwdriver into the electrical breaker panel which sent a shower of sparks, the likes of which have not been seen except on the fourth of July, across the cabin of the boat. The crew quickly recognized the limitations of Eric's handy work and agreed that the broken air conditioner would probably be fine for the night and they returned to the *Bagheera*.

Without even asking Eric and John what their plans were, the Dutch rescuers had set up a bunk in an air conditioned cabin for them to sleep that night. To show his appreciation, John broke out his rum bottle from the *Soggy Dollar Bar*, upgrading the party from beer to rum. The drinks and laughs lasted well into the early morning hours. At one hazy point, both John and Eric stumbled into their comfortable cabin and slept like babies.

The Next Morning

They woke before anyone else in the quiet, cool cabin on the *Bagheera* with fuzzy memories of the night before. The soft sound of the boat's generator was like a jackhammer in their heads. In the sleepy harbour of West End the sun was shining, the temperature was mild, and the water was smooth as glass. They immediately went to work in the galley cleaning the pile of dirty dishes from the night before. They figured it was the least they could do.

As a few other people slowly made their way to the deck, one of the Dutch guys helped Eric offload his kayak from the yacht and put it back into the water. He then helped with their bags and souvenirs, loading them into the dinghy he had used to take them ashore. John and Eric never got the opportunity to say goodbye to most of the Dutch airline gang. But given the previous night's events, the rest of the group likely wouldn't be coming up for daylight any time soon.

Eric, John, and the hung-over Dutchman quietly powered past the slumbering, pristine white yachts and polished teak sailboats to the back part of the harbour, where the scene quickly became more derelict, littered with many abandoned boats and vessels under repair.

He dropped off the two Americans and one kayak and turned the dinghy back out towards the *Bagheera*. Eric called me to check my status and give me an update of what their plans were. They decided Eric would hit up the small market to resupply his kayak and then head out to rendezvous with me at Cinnamon Bay, St. John. John's plan was to catch the ferry to St. John to meet up with us there.

John

With very little baggage John opted to walk around to the ferry dock. It was about a half a mile walk, but a refreshing one, and it helped to work out any remnants of the residual morning hangover. In addition, it was a beautiful tropical morning and he, after all, had nothing but time. The small harbour town was just beginning to come to life for the day as John made his way around West End.

The ferry station was basically empty except for a few straggling workers or wandering locals. John purchased his five dollar ticket to Cruz Bay, St. John, but the boat wouldn't depart for a few hours, so he spent the remainder of the morning in a nearby restaurant enjoying the scenery and an early lunch.

In the meantime, and, after saying goodbye to John, Eric set off to prepare to join me. He walked in to the lone decrepit market to purchase some food and water. The man behind the counter informed him they had a very limited supply of water and it was already spoken for. Eric's frustration must have been apparent because the man relented and sold him two gallons.

About that time, Eric's consumption from the previous night began to catch up. His gut began to bubble. Nature was calling and did not care if Eric was ready or not. Sweat formed on his forehead as he asked the man if he could use the restroom. As further evidence of God's sense of humor, Eric was informed the store did not have running water, therefore no restroom he could use. He grabbed his two gallons of water and did a clenched-ass speed shuffle back down to his boat where he tossed the jugs into the sand. At a full run he began dropping his shorts before he ever made the tree line. Anyone within eyesight had to be either cracking up or scratching their heads. In a last minute, desperation leap that could have made ESPN's top 10 plays of the day, he landed in the protection of a cluster of trees as nature took its course.

He emerged a brand new man. He had a beautiful morning to paddle, he had restored his water rations, and he was a few pounds lighter. With no pressure and plenty of time, Eric inspected his boat in the sand. He was concerned the drunken

Dutchman method of kayak hoisting may have caused a few issues. Hanging eighteen feet of fully loaded kayak by D rings that were glued on was a gutsy maneuver. Fortunately, there was no obvious damage. So, with renewed optimism, Eric paddled out into West End Harbour.

He paddled for a few hundred yards when he noticed water quickly filling his boat. More so than ever before. Frustration returned by kicking optimism's ass. He began to realize he was by himself; he could repair what he *hoped* was the only problem, and then would have to paddle back across the perilous waters that brought him to Tortola.

Eric turned around to return to shore. He was about twenty feet from the shore when his bright orange kayak became a bright orange submarine. The weight of the water had dropped the combing of the cockpit below the waterline and had effectively sunk his boat. The cumulative anger from the entire boat building process and the trip had reached an apex. Eric shouted an expletive that begins with "f" and ends with "uck" informing the entire harbour he was less than happy.

Eric rolled out of his kayak and began dragging what felt like the sunken *Titanic* back to shore. His struggles garnered the attention of a local passerby who waded into the water and helped them back to shore.

Eric needed to reset. He called John, not knowing where he was at the time, and said his boat was taking on water, he was pissed, and he was done for the day. He would need a few hours to take everything apart and then he would join John on the ferry to St. John. John informed him his ferry was about to leave so the best option would be for Eric to catch the next one. There was one slight problem. Eric had no money or credit cards and was on a foreign island with a broken boat.

John said not to sweat it, he would buy Eric a ferry ticket, and get him a cab. John approached the less than friendly immigrations government worker. I think "less than friendly" is actually a job requirement for those in Customs and Immigration. If, when applying for the job, the applicant smiles at any point during the interview process, they are instantly removed from consideration. John explained the situation and said he wanted to purchase a ticket for his friend who would be there in a few hours. "He is a big white guy with a big moustache. He'll have a heavy black duffel bag and will most likely be in a really bad mood." With John's insistence, the official relented and agreed to take the money. All John could do was trust her and hope she didn't just pocket the cash.

The next problem was transportation. John walked out of the ticket station and found a few island cabbies milling around. He, again, explained what was going on and was forced to reiterate to one of the drivers what he wanted. "I want to pay you now to go to the market around the harbour in two hours, pick up my friend and his bags, and bring him back here." Again, with blind faith, John handed the man his money.

John called Eric and told him all arrangements had been made. That was all he could do. John's next action made the finality of his surrender all the more real: he called his wife. He told her he was fine but everything had come undone, and he would need a hotel booked on St. John. Within a few minutes she had booked a reservation at the Westin on St. John. He boarded the ferry and enjoyed the beautiful ride back to U.S. territory.

Eric

In two hours, right on schedule, the taxi showed up to pick up Eric. The giant duffel bag of kayak along with all of his other gear was loaded up into the cab and, without a single issue, they drove to the ferry dock where the ticket John had purchased was there and waiting for him. Like John before him, Eric had some time to kill, so he walked down to a restaurant where he sat and plotted out how he would repair his boat, rent a powerboat, and go get what was left of John's boat on Great Thatch to fix it up. Eric clearly had not yet surrendered. The trip, in his mind, was merely delayed. He called John and found out about the hotel reservations on St. John. Everything was coming back together. Again.

The time had come to board the ferry and Eric was adjusting his things. As he stepped onto the boat he heard a slight but definite "plop". Only mildly concerned, he located a spot on the boat and kicked back to enjoy the ride over. It wasn't until St. John came into sight and he began to think about calling John to give him an update that, in a moment of clarity, he realized what had happened. The "plop" he had heard at the ferry dock sounded much like a "plop" would sound if a cell phone fell into the water creating a "plop". His cell phone was at the bottom of the Caribbean Sea.

CHAPTER 10

Coming Apart and Coming Together

Meanwhile, on Great Thatch Island, the bright glow of the morning sun filtered through the ceiling of leaves and branches above me. It was about 5:30 a.m. when my eyelids reluctantly lifted. For anyone who suffers from insomnia, I suggest complete exhaustion with a touch of rum for a getting a good night's sleep. I was refreshed and with the sun shining brightly, I immediately recognized the potential of the day. As the fragrances of morning and sea air filled my senses, so my thoughts began to fill with optimism. I began to wonder where the other guys were, where we might be able to meet up, and what kind of condition John's boat was in. Then my thoughts turned to my own boat. Boat... My boat... MY BOAT!

I sat up, grabbed my knife, and ran down to the beach, fearing that my kayak had decided to venture out on its own and leave me to live out the rest of my days in a secluded paradise, wishing to God I had packed more toothpaste. Thankfully, my boat was right where I left it! I stopped in my tracks and gave a huge sigh of relief. My boat and I had made it through the night. Things were certainly looking up. This morning was the first time in the past eighteen hours I was able to take some time to be happy and enjoy my surroundings. The sun was shining, the sky was blue, the water was calm, and I had my boat and nothing but time.

By all accounts it was a perfect morning. I looked around and tried to once again take in the beauty of the islands. The sun had just climbed over the eastern part of Great Thatch. St. John, directly to the south, was shrouded in morning haze; and the more distant islands and cays were mere suggestions of land in the distance.

During this moment of morning bliss, something caught my eye. About forty yards to my left was my paddle nestled gently in the sand right where I initially had come to shore the night before. I immediately had a flashback of hitting the beach in the rain and throwing my paddle on the shore before I hopped out of my kayak, dropped into the sand, and performed what I affectionately called a "Technicolor yawn." I had no clue how, throughout the turbulent night, the tide had not pulled it into the ocean and into an abyss to never be seen again. It then dawned on me what a stupid mistake I had made leaving it there, and how devastating it would have been to lose my paddle. Stupid!!! Once again, someone up above was looking out for me.

I quickly but carefully broke down camp, taking special care to pack correctly. I had recently learned the benefits of having a flashlight, knife, food, and water within reach. The red top of my kayak was unzipped and laid open like a fish recently filleted. I was stuffing my things into the open skeleton of the boat when I received a phone call from Eric who said they had spent the night on the yacht. I imagined they were all too drunk to try to pull safely in to any marina, so they slept it off.

Eric and John had been brought to Tortola and safely dropped off by the charitable Dutch pilots. They were formulating a plan on what to do about their respective kayaks and how and where to meet back up with me. I told Eric that I would be departing Great Thatch soon. My plan was to cross to St. John and travel along the coast until I reached Cinnamon Bay. I would then pay for a campground, set up camp, and wait to hear from them. With any luck I would still have a signal.

There were a few minor complications. Technically we were all in a foreign country. I was going to paddle illegally back to a United States territory without clearing customs. Eric planned to do the same and John would have to catch a ferry back and legally check in with Customs and Immigration. He said he would call me right back and let me know their plan to get John back to the U.S. and Eric and his kayak to me. We had made a mess of things, and were making plans to clean it up.

I hung up the phone with reclaimed confidence. There was swagger in my stride. The weather and water were in my favor; and I had been transformed from a trespassing stranger, struggling to find a safe place to catch his breath the night before to a survivor, an explorer, with a plan for moving forward. I was re-inspired. For the moment anyway. I walked the beach for about forty minutes waiting for the call. Having heard nothing, I became impatient and decided it was time to go.

As I approached the kayak, my phone rang. Eric told me he would load up his boat and head for Cinnamon Bay to meet me. John was going to take the ferry to Cruz Bay, St. John and then maybe catch a cab to Cinnamon Bay. Once we were all on St. John, we would figure out what to do next. We had a plan. I turned off my phone, put it safely in the dry bag, and took one last look at the island to try and capture it in my mind. It had become my respite from the chaos, my shelter, and my home for one night.

I could feel the affable warmth of the morning sun on my shoulders and the soft breeze that was blowing across my face. It was euphoric. Even with the sound of water rolling on to the shore, the island was tranquil and quiet. I closed my eyes and tried to hold on to that feeling of serenity.

Back to Business

I walked my kayak down the sand and into the ocean. The once difficult entry into the boat had become an action without thought. I waited for a wave to pass. On the back side of the wave, I placed one leg into the cockpit. With my hands on the gunwales I stiffened my arms, raised my body up while maintaining balance, and eased myself past the combing and into the cockpit. Funny that only a few days ago that action was awkward and difficult. It had quickly become a smooth and flawless operation. As I paddled out to sea, the ache in my muscles had awakened. The little muscles in my hands and feet and in weird places in my back were crying out to let me know that they were not used to the kinds of repetitive motions I had required of them the day before.

The further from shore I paddled, the more I started to remember how deceiving the water can be. When you are basically eye level with the water, there are no subtleties. Even the smallest lift in the water, every rise and fall, is magnified. St. John was becoming closer with every stroke and the lactic acid was being forced out of my muscles. The pain subsided as I turned to the west and began to move parallel to the coast.

The morning sun rose quickly and the air was becoming warmer. The coast to my left was beautiful but unfriendly. It was lined with jagged rocks that climbed sometimes forty or fifty feet out of the water. The water seemed to hate these rocks because of the constant barrage it was placing against them. As I approached these points, my anxiety rose in proportion with the restlessness of the water. I was forced to be more aware of the incoming wave sets. The waves were big enough that if I was hit broadside I would be in big trouble. My boat would capsize and I would be in treacherous water with no way out. There were several times I had to point my kayak away from shore and face the open ocean in order to head into especially large waves so as not to get rolled. I paddled extra hard to get beyond these points.

My destination was the campground at Cinnamon Bay. Without a map, I was navigating from memory alone. There are no signs out at sea and no gas stations to stop and ask for directions. (Not that I, as a man, would do so even if they were available.) I was expecting to paddle about an hour before I reached Cinnamon Bay. But, again, that was a blind guess.

The Struggle

An hour came and went. I had surpassed the jagged, rocky coastline and was approaching more hospitable terrain. Each bay I came upon looked beautiful, but did not look quite like Cinnamon Bay as I had remembered. Hope unfurled in my chest with each new inlet, and disappointment showed up and kicked hope in the ass. So I continued telling myself that it must be the next bay. ...or the next bay. ...or the next bay.

After paddling for several hours I became increasingly skeptical and frustrated. My body started to ache again. My muscles were fatigued. My lungs hurt from sucking wind for hours. My legs were numb and my core had been held all morning. The "fun" was virtually gone from this trip. The islands seemed to be mocking me. The water was no longer beautiful, but a constant challenge: a foe who was out to get me. I was beginning to feel like a mad man. I would talk out loud to myself when the challenges became severe. As I was getting pushed towards the shore or see rocks just below the surface I would say out loud, "Come on, come on, come on!" "Not the rocks, not the rocks!" (Repetitive comments are an unconscious reaction to stressful situations. If you do not believe me, watch the dog fight scenes in *Top Gun*. The script reads something like this: "Look out! Look out!" "There he is! There he is!" "I got him! I got him!") When I was at my most frustrated, I would talk to the water. Through clenched teeth I would growl, "You will NOT get me! Not today!" I'm laughing as I type this because I remember all too well the clash of fear and bravado.

To this day I do not know exactly where I was when I decided I had to get to shore. I had taken on too much water and needed to rest. Hours of constant paddling had taken its toll. I approached what I thought could be a safe place. About twenty yards off shore, I was made painfully aware of what John had experienced the day before. The current was pushing me towards the land, and rocks were waiting just below the surface. It was too late to back out, and too rocky to land. I did my best to stealthily maneuver around the subsurface rocks that seemed intent on ripping a hole in my boat and in my spirit.

When I was close enough that I started to drag, I hopped out of the boat. I held it in place; and as waves approached, I walked my boat with the wave until it touched rock again. I then stopped and waited for the next wave. I repeated this movement, effectively hopping my boat over the rocks with the assistance of the waves, until I was on shore.

As soon as I safely reached land, however, I realized that the same waves that had safely brought me to shore, now had me pinned. I would not be able to get out again against the constant barrage of incoming waves. I was furious. I wanted to quit. I wanted to leave the boat right where it was and walk away. I could find a road somewhere up on the shore and hitch a ride to the nearest hotel. I could be in an air conditioned room with a comfortable bed in no time. But I had not come that far for the story to end that way. I sat on the shore in an attempt to regain feeling in my legs. Once I had rested sufficiently, I walked around the beach a little. Actually, I was pacing. I knew St. John was a very populated island and I was safe, but it was the principle of the thing. I was not going to leave my boat on that rocky shore and go for help. I would make it to the finish line. This had become a game that I had resolved to win.

Determined to triumph over the elements, I pumped the water out of my boat and reversed my previous walk over the waves and into the water. As expected, that proved to be much more difficult than bringing it in. I was going the wrong way down a one way street. I had to get the kayak out far enough to be off the rocks, but shallow enough that I could re-enter it without flipping it over. I knew as soon as I left my feet, the boat would be pushed back into the rocks. It had to be a quick, fluid motion. Very quick. And very fluid. I was ready to try but I needed a whole lot of luck. I counted down and chickened out several times. Once I mustered up the guts to take my shot, I saw my window of opportunity, hopped in, and in a quick awkward movement started paddling like I had never paddled before to get off the rocks before they ripped a hole in my hull. I crept over the incoming waves, around the rocks and out into the ocean. I was paddling against the grain. It felt like running sprints in a pool, but I had done it.

The weight of the entire plan going to shit was heavy on my mind, body, and spirit. I was running on fumes in every possible way. I paddled out to sea, still in search of Cinnamon Bay. The sun's rays were intensifying. I worked my way around to the next bay, only to find myself in a similar situation. This time I stayed far enough away from the shore to keep myself in the water. But I needed to find sand and soon. I was beginning to feel defeated and was seriously wanting to throw in the towel and stop. I rounded what I would later find out was Hawksnest Bay and wandered into Caneel Bay, and there it was. If it wasn't an illusion, I was looking at powdery sand with not a single soul in sight. It was a beautiful beach and I needed to get to it. I paddled hard at the shore and slid my kayak up on to the beach. I pushed and dragged it as far up on shore as I could. I tied it to a tree and, as my new tradition would dictate, I dropped to my ass and sat in the sand for a few minutes.

The Bubble Bursts and the Struggle Continues

I needed to find out just where I was and how far away I was from Cinnamon Bay. I walked up on land and found myself on the property of some resort that appeared to be closed for the season.   There was a man working on the landscaping and I explained to him that I had just beached my boat and was looking for Cinnamon Bay. "Oh, Cinnamon bay's not far. Just a couple of bays over," he informed me and pointed to his right in EXACTLY the direction from which I had just come. I had missed it. I had paddled for my life a quarter of the way around the island PAST where I needed to be. I could feel a wave of anger sweep over me. I asked if he had a map of St. John that I could see. I needed visual conformation of where I was, where I wanted to be, and just what in the hell I had just done to myself. His hospitality had expired, unfortunately. He told me that he did not have a map and that I was trespassing and should get off the property. I just thought to myself, "Yep, that's about right."

I walked back down to the beach in defeat. I had been fighting for my life at multiple times throughout the morning, and I was tired of paddling. Cinnamon Bay had the only legal campground I knew of, so I needed to get there. I needed to get out of my boat for a day or so and decide what to do with my remaining time in the islands. Only a few days prior, all I wanted to do was explore the islands in my kayak. Standing in the sand of Caneel Bay, a picturesque tropical paradise, all I could think was how much I did not want to get back in that boat.

With no energy or motivation, I pushed back out to sea and headed back the way I had come. This was the worst journey to date. I was tired. I was angry. I was doubling back on the way I had come in hopes I would land in the bay that I had already passed once. Literally, each stroke was a struggle. I paddled back past Hawksnest Bay and headed for a beautiful post card beach that had to be Cinnamon Bay. Everything in me wanted to quit, but I kept telling myself that with each paddle the end was closer. The shore was just beyond my reach but was getting bigger by the second. The last hundred yards was the absolute worst. Just like the last hour of a long road trip, it was torturous. I could feel my muscles wanting to quit. But the magnetic draw of the finish line kept me in motion. Left, right, left, right. The rhythm quickened. "Sprint to the finish line", I thought to myself. I hit the beach, hopped out and breathed a huge sigh of relief. I was done! I was there! I did not have to paddle any more unless I wanted to. Thank God! A pregnant woman who was picking up seashells came walking by. I asked her, just for confirmation, "Is this Cinnamon Bay?" What happened next is a blur, but I'm pretty sure I heard the words, "No, this is Trunk Bay. Cinnamon Bay is the next bay over." It felt like a boulder had landed on my head. I don't think I even thanked her or asked for confirmation; I simply pushed my boat back out, hopped in, and started paddling with an anger I had never known before. I was furious. God has a sense of humor, I thought, and I was the punch line that day.

Cinnamon Bay

I left Trunk Bay and rounded the point toward the next bay, and, within about thirty minutes, I turned my kayak toward the next beach. I recognized the rock formation in the middle of the bay named Mary Point. I remembered it from when I passed it the first time TWO HOURS prior to that. I remember thinking I no longer cared if it was Cinnamon Bay or not. I was done paddling. My kayak slid up into the sand, I climbed out of my boat, and threw my paddle in frustrated anger up toward the trees. I was pissed. I was tired and more than anything, I was DONE. A local man walked by, wearing low hanging, yet extremely short shorts and dreadlocks that were halfway down his back. As he passed I asked (not really caring at that point) if it was Cinnamon Bay. He nodded and gave an affirming "yes." I threw my head up towards the sky and took a deep breath. I looked back at him as he walked about ten steps past me, faced the woods, and starting peeing right there on the beach. Nice.

It didn't matter. I had arrived at Cinnamon Bay. I had made it. After taking a few minutes to catch my breath and get my legs under me, I walked up the path leading from the beach to the building that houses the gift shop, diner, and the camp site office. I was eager to get my campsite picked out, so I could pitch my tent and start relaxing. With each step I began to feel more accomplished and less angry. My new goal was to get a "legal" place to camp and then find out where Eric and John were. It occurred to me that until then, the other two guys had not crossed my mind once the entire day. I walked up the paved path that led from the beach, up through the campsites, and to a check-in booth/snack shop. The first thing I did was order two cans of Coke and a Whatchamacallit candy bar. Don't judge me. My choices were very limited. As the unfriendly woman behind the counter was digging my candy bar out of the cooler, my eyes wandered to a sign posted to my right. *"Campground will be closed through October. Will open again November 1st"* I stood there in shock, unable to move or speak. Time stopped.

I stared at the sign in disbelief, recalling the harrowing events of the day: I had paddled extremely difficult water well PAST Cinnamon Bay, then finding out my mistake, paddled across the rough water BACK to Cinnamon Bay for the sole purpose of getting to a campground to find it was CLOSED?!? I opened up my first can of Coke and drank it down. It burned my dry throat, but it was cold and it was delicious. I threw the can away in surrender. This was the end of the kayak trip for me.

Breaking Down

I noticed a line of wheelbarrows all chained together and secured with a padlock. I asked one of the passing maintenance men if I could borrow or even rent a wheelbarrow. I was going to break down my kayak on the beach, wheel it up, throw it in a cab, and head for a hotel in Cruz Bay. He said he did not have a key, but would drive his truck down and pick me up. Even better. Thank you!

I strolled back down toward the beach with an arrogant air about me. Someone could have come and put a gun in my face and I would have smiled, stuck my finger in the barrel cartoon style, and said "pull the trigger." The kayak trip was over. The conclusion of the trip was almost cathartic. I truly had not a care in the world. I was on dry land. I did not have to worry about the weather, a schedule, packing, unpacking, repacking, replacing, misplacing, or where I tucked my toilet paper. Life was easy again. The ocean had not beaten me. The sun was shining, and I had nowhere to go and no one to be.

Tourists gave me sideways looks from their reclined positions on comfortable beach chairs as I took apart my boat on their, otherwise, pristine beach. I felt like I was a pimple on the face of Mona Lisa. People appeared angry with me for tainting their view. Once again, I did not care. I maintained the arrogance and a smile that kept me above everyone and everything else. I would take a section apart, rinse it in the ocean, and then place it across a dead tree to dry. I maintained my cocky swagger, almost daring someone to approach me and question me or tell me I couldn't be there. It took me about two hours to take the kayak apart and rinse, dry, and repack everything.

Next Step - Find the Other Guys

As I was finishing up, a man and a woman came motoring up in a big, yellow, inflatable rented dinghy. I could tell it was a rental because of the sharp eye for water craft I had developed over the past few days. ...that, and the giant "RENT ME" painted on both sides. They were on the beach, but barely, when they started to get out. Experience is a funny thing. A little goes a long way. I had been a sea kayaker for the grand total of five days, but I had picked up a few things. I hollered out to the guy with confidence, "You're too close to the water. You better push it up further." He smiled a friendly smile and said, "Naa, I think we're high and dry." With the smugness of someone who had been raised on those waters, I said, "For now," and then turned back to packing my kayak bag. I felt cocky and sure of myself.

The tide was coming in and with each wave, I knew it would be under his boat within the hour. The couple walked away from me and down the beach hand in hand. I kept a watchful eye on their boat as I took mine apart. And, of course, within fifteen minutes the rental was being slowly reclaimed by the ocean. I caught him out of the corner of my eye running back to the boat. I smiled and walked over and grabbed the side of the boat as it was now floating in the shallow surf. Together we walked it back to the shore. He did not say a word other than "thank you," but I knew he felt a little bit embarrassed.

He and his wife decided they would just go ahead and shove off. As I helped them into their boat they asked about my kayak. I gave them a brief version of our story and told them I had no cell signal and no real idea where my friends were. They offered me use of their cell phone. I declined at first and then realized it was no time for pride. I accepted their offer. I called Eric first, not knowing at the time his phone was at the bottom of the ocean. I then called John who answered and told me he was at the Westin on St. John. No other statement could have made me as elated as that one did. We were on the same island and he already had a first class hotel room. Say no more. Destination: the Westin! I thanked the couple, who I learned were on vacation from Arkansas, and shoved them off the sand. We exchanged waves, and they motored away.

I walked back up the path to find the guy with the truck. He saw me first and shouted out, "You ready?" I hopped into the back, and we headed down to the beach. He helped me load my bags into the bed and delivered me back up to a waiting taxi.

Sweet, Sweet Civilization

My bags and I were delivered to John's doorstep at the Westin. I walked into the room and felt like collapsing onto the bed. I dragged my bag inside the room and leaned back against the door as it closed. The adventure was over. It was time to relax and start to enjoy things again. John asked if I was mad at them. I told him, of course, I wasn't mad; I was just tired and beat up.

I took a long, much needed shower. I stood under the hot water for probably thirty minutes. My aching body needed it as well as my beat up mind. After getting out and drying off, I put on clean (which is a relative term at that point of the trip) clothes. I then laid down on the king sized bed and, without consciously thinking about it, closed my eyes. It actually hurt to close them. They were stinging in painful ecstasy. It felt so good.

John said he had talked to Eric who was still on Tortola but would be on the 4:00 ferry to St. John. It was already about 2:00, so we caught a cab to Cruz Bay to wait for him. Once we were dropped off near the ferry dock, John and I wandered into *Woody's Saloon* (a local favorite) and ordered blackened Mahi sandwiches and a couple of beers. Each bite of the sandwich was better than the previous one. It felt gluttonous. The beer was cold and delicious. You would have thought we were refugees who had been in a prison camp for years, the way we were devouring it all. Once we were satisfactorily full, we wandered down to *Margarita Phil's* for a change of scenery and a few more beverages while we waited for Eric.

Reunited

Right on schedule, Eric arrived on the 4:00 ferry. A wave of relief washed over me seeing him climb off of that ferry boat along with a few dozen other passengers. We were all three back together. We exchanged hugs and agreed to save story time for later. John gave Eric a room key, and he took a cab to the Westin to unload his stuff. John and I continued to sample adult beverages in bar-rich Cruz Bay. About an hour later, Eric resurfaced and caught up with John and me at the *Quiet Mon Pub* which is situated right next door to *Woody's*, where we began the evening.

John, Eric, and I spent the remainder of the evening drinking, laughing, and drinking some more. We told stories of turbulent seas, deserted islands, and Dutch airline pilots. The challenges, fear, and frustrations of the previous days had disappeared. We deserved that release. We became blissfully and completely drunk.

We had done it! We had a vision. We set a goal. We built boats. We came to the Virgin Islands. We found adventure. We took a trip that most would never dream of taking (granted, for good reason). Most importantly, we survived to tell the story. On an island in one of the most beautiful places in the world, we were all alive and toasting everything we could think of as the rounds kept coming. We stepped out of our respective comfort zones and stepped into the ring with Mother Nature. With a fresh perspective, an unquestionable respect for the ocean, and a renewed sense of self, we came out on the other side as better men. That night, overlooking the street below on an outside deck of *The Quiet Mon* we were not toasting ourselves but the good life. The life not spent in the confines of the subdivision. That night and again tonight as I write this I give a toast: to those who dare to venture from the routine existence that shackles so many. Here's to those who aren't satisfied with going to see the mountain, but who need to experience it, experience it with all of their senses: feeling it against their skin as they climb, smelling it on the way up, and seeing the view from the top.

Here's to three fools from Kansas who dreamed to build boats and take them across the ocean...and did it.

CHAPTER 11

What a Long, Strange Trip It's Been

I suppose I should tell you how the last few days of our time in the islands were spent. Eric, John, and I stayed just that one night at the Westin on St. John. We came back from our night of drinking completely fall-down drunk. Sleeping arrangements had to be decided in the room where there was a king sized bed and a pull-out couch. Just like at Ivan's Stress Free Campground on Jost Van Dyke, we threw rock, paper, scissors to see who would get the pull out-couch, but would sleep alone while the other two shared the bed. I won't say that I "won," but I slept alone while they slept together. Again.

Knowing we could not afford to stay there any longer, we packed our bags and headed into Cruz Bay, St. John where Eric and I mailed our kayaks back home. We were forced to procure random cardboard boxes from tourist shops throughout Cruz Bay in order to get all of our things shipped back. We learned you can actually mail a canvas bag full of boat parts with little resistance. We also learned that after lugging an 80 pound bag in and out of cabs and ferry boats for a week, money becomes no object. We walked into the post office with complete and overwhelming apathy. When the slightly annoyed man behind the counter weighed our bags, we could not have cared less about the total dollar amount. No cost was too great to relinquish ourselves of the burden of those heavy bags. I placed my credit card on the counter and felt the weight of the world lift from my shoulders as he placed the $70 postage stamp on my salty, weathered canvas bag.

   With no more kayaks to drag around, we walked over to *Woody's* for one last blackened Mahi sandwich and a couple of beers. We then headed down to the ferry, bought our five dollar tickets, and blended in with the dozens of other tourists who were also cruising across to Red Hook, St. Thomas. Most of them left their resort for the day to come over to St. John to do some shopping and sight-seeing. The three of us had been at battle for the past week. We must have looked like it too. In most ways, we were no different than the other tourists on the ferry, but, because of what we had experienced the past week, we were vastly different. Not better - but certainly different.

   From the Red Hook ferry dock we took a cab to Bolongo Bay where Eric's wife Erin would be meeting up with him to celebrate their anniversary. John and I considered asking if we could crash with them, but did not want to face the certain rejection, so we opted to get our own room.

   After Erin's arrival, Eric came up with the idea we could rent a boat and head back over to salvage some of John's things. So, on our last full day in the islands together, we headed back in to Red Hook and rented a boat. Eric was the captain and motored us out across the ocean. Erin sat alone in the back taking in the scenery while John and I moved around the boat viewing the waters with different eyes. I looked down as we cruised right over the waves and realized that prior to this trip, I would have said the sea seemed relatively calm. Now, with the education of experience, I saw the ocean as a kayaker and noticed the true texture of it: every swell and drop. To this day, I am still amazed how differently I view the ocean. The three of us had acquired an overwhelming respect for the power of the ocean, and it was palpable in the unspoken words as we cruised towards St. John.

Before *Operation: Salvage John's Crap* we decided to stop at Water Lemon Cay in Leinster Bay, St. John to snorkel a bit. We saw dozens of starfish, abundant sea life, and even a reef shark. It was the relaxation and fun we needed. That stop transformed the Virgin Islands into a vacation destination again.

After a brief recess, we continued over to the north side of Great Thatch where John and I swam ashore and salvaged some of his things. It was sad to leave his kayak there on that island, but we really had no choice. It is possibly still there to this day. E-mail me and I'll get you the GPS coordinates.

We spent the remainder of the day on Jost Van Dyke where we stopped in at the *Soggy Dollar Bar* in White Bay and then made a brief return visit to *Foxy's* in Great Harbour. The weather was warm. The water was clear. The drinks were cold and savory. It all added up to the perfect ending to the adventure. As Eric navigated us back west towards Red Hook that evening, I could feel the imminent end of the trip. We didn't speak the entire ride back. The sun was setting on the day and on our visit.

I previously mentioned that when you travel, the story of who you were becomes the story of who you are. The men that walked in to John's garage the previous year, with a toolbox and an idea, were not the same men that were driving a boat into the sunset that evening through Pilsbury Sound in the U.S. Virgin Islands. Experience had changed us. There were no major personal transformations or significant lifestyle adjustments. The differences were found in the subtleties: we laughed harder, the ties of our friendships felt stronger, stress seemed more manageable, and the little things were just that - little things. But more than anything else, I think we discovered that life is more than a career and responsibilities. We found life just beyond the boundaries of our own comfort. It was in the trials and triumphs, in the successes and failures. It was in a basic reliance on our fellow man as well as the natural elements. F. Scott Fitzgerald wrote, "Our lives are determined by opportunities, even ones we miss." Eric, John, and I challenged ourselves and, although it didn't turn out exactly the way we intended, we returned as better men.

THE END

I want to thank you for reading along and taking this journey with us. This story, with the exception of Chapter 9, has been told from MY perspective. John and Eric could write their own books about the journey from their view, and these may be completely different than my own. We are all fortunate enough to have friends in life. I am happy to say that I have many great friends that I care about deeply. But only these few could and would go on a trip like this one and make it the adventure it became. We quite literally rolled with the ebb and flow. We managed to laugh with each other and at each other beyond every obstacle. There were times we were ready to kill each other, but at the end of the day we were in each other's corner. Fellas, we toasted with Cruzan bottles on the beach of Brewer's Bay, Tortola to kick it off and celebrated the end with rum drinks at *The Quiet Mon* in Cruz Bay, St. John. Thanks for having my back as we challenged ourselves and the unknown and for taking the brotherhood we live to the next level. Even though we questioned our sanity over and over again throughout the entire journey, we fucking did it.

To see pictures and video of this journey visit
www.scottfinazzo.com.

Acknowledgements

The families: Amy, Ryan, Nick, and Cameron Finazzo, Erin and Zach Gifford, Vickie, Katie, and Bailey Heffernon.

Thank you: Keith Murry, our OPFD family, my parents, my brothers and sisters, WeissenFinazOpezMcRobJaegDietWinks for being the best family, influence, and support team a man could have, Stacy Judy, Jacqueline Nelson for the hard work and positive support, Scott B. Williams for being a friend, a mentor, and unknowingly planting the seed, Hyon Min Han and Melissa LaVigne for opening a door that cannot be closed.

Finally, to John Heffernon and Eric Gifford - my brothers. Who's better than us tonight?

Printed in Great Britain
by Amazon.co.uk, Ltd.,
Marston Gate.